classic
puddings & pies

classic
puddings & pies

TRADITIONAL RECIPES FOR DELECTABLE DESSERTS

MARTHA DAY

HERMES
HOUSE

This edition is published by Hermes House

Hermes House is an imprint of Anness Publishing Ltd
Hermes House, 88–89 Blackfriars Road, London SE1 8HA
tel. 020 7401 2077; fax 020 7633 9499; info@anness.com

© Anness Publishing Ltd 1994, 2004

A CIP catalogue record for this book is available from the British Library

Publisher: Joanna Lorenz
Editor: Linda Fraser
Designers: Tony Paine and Roy Prescott
Photographers: Steve Baxter, Karl Adamson and Amanda Heywood
Food for Photography: Wendy Lee, Jane Stevenson and Elizabeth Wolf-Choen

Front cover: William Lingwood, Photographer;
Helen Trent, Stylist; Sunil Vijayakar, Home Economist

Previously Published as *Creative Cooking Library: Traditional Puddings & Pies*

1 3 5 7 9 10 8 6 4 2

Measurements
For all recipes, quantities are given in both metric and imperial measures and, where appropriate, measures are also
given in standard cups and spoons. Follow one set, but not a mixture because they are not interchangeable.

CONTENTS

INTRODUCTION

Home-made puddings, pies and tarts are a pleasure to make and delicious to eat. There are recipes here for every occasion throughout the year – you'll find puddings suitable for special celebrations and family meals, too. When you are planning a meal, the choice of the other courses is important; for instance, you might choose a light main course to go with a rich creamy dessert or a sweet and filling pie, or pick something hearty to go with one of the simpler, fruit desserts. If you are planning a festive meal or a party, make sure

you leave plenty of time for preparation – and do some of the work ahead of time if you can. Pastry, for instance, can be made a day or two in advance and chilled until ready to use, or even frozen for up to 3 months if you are really organized! All the recipes have step-by-step instructions, and in this section you'll find special tips and techniques to help you make perfect egg custard, simple meringue and fruit sauces, as well as helpful hints on preparing the pastry and decorations for pies and tarts.

MAKING CUSTARD

A home-made custard is a luscious sauce for many hot and cold puddings. The secret for success is patience. Don't try to hurry the cooking of the custard by raising the heat.

Makes about 450ml/¾ pint

450ml/¾ pint milk
1 vanilla pod, split in half
4 egg yolks
45–60ml/3–4 tbsp caster sugar,
   to sprinkle

1 Put the milk in a heavy-based saucepan. Hold the vanilla pod over the pan and scrape out the tiny black seeds into the milk. Add the split pod to the milk.

2 Heat the milk until bubbles appear round the edge. Remove from the heat, cover and set aside to infuse for 10 minutes. Remove the split vanilla pod.

3 In a bowl, lightly beat the egg yolks with the sugar until smoothly blended and creamy. Gradually add the hot milk to the egg yolks, stirring constantly.

6 Strain the custard into a bowl. If using cold, sprinkle a little caster sugar over the surface of the custard to help prevent a skin from forming. Set the bowl in a container of iced water and leave to cool.

4 Pour the mixture into the top of a double boiler (or a bowl). Set over the bottom pan containing hot water. Put on a moderately low heat, so the water stays below the boil.

VARIATIONS

● Use 5ml/1 tsp vanilla essence instead of the vanilla pod. Omit steps 1 and 2, and add the essence after straining the custard.
● For Chocolate Custard add 50g/2oz plain chocolate, grated, to the hot milk and sugar mixture. Stir until smooth before adding to the egg yolks.

5 Cook, stirring constantly, for 10–12 minutes or until the custard thickens to a creamy consistency that will coat the spoon. Immediately remove the pan or bowl of custard from over the pan of hot water.

DAMAGE REPAIR

If the custard gets too hot and starts to curdle, remove it from the heat immediately and pour it into a bowl. Whisk vigorously for 2–3 seconds or until smooth. Then pour it back into the pan and continue cooking.

MAKING A FRUIT SAUCE

A smooth, uncooked fruit sauce, called a 'coulis' in French, has a refreshing flavour and beautiful colour. You can use fresh or frozen fruit for the sauce. If using frozen fruit, partially thaw and drain on kitchen paper before puréeing.

Makes about 250ml/8fl oz

450g/1lb raspberries, strawberries or
   blackberries
25–50g/1–2oz/3–6 tbsp icing sugar,
   sifted
squeeze of lemon juice (optional)
15–30ml/1–2 tbsp Kirsch or fruit
   liqueur (optional)

1 Hull the berries if necessary. Put them in a bowl of cold water and swirl them round briefly. Scoop out and spread on kitchen paper. Pat dry. Purée the berries in a blender or food processor. Turn the machine on and off a few times and scrape down the bowl to be sure all the berries are evenly puréed.

2 For raspberries, blackberries and other berries with small seeds, press the purée through a fine-mesh nylon sieve. Add icing sugar to taste, plus a little lemon juice and/or liqueur, if using (for example, choose raspberry liqueur, or *framboise*, for a raspberry sauce). Stir well to dissolve the sugar completely.

MAKING SIMPLE MERINGUE

This soft meringue is used as a topping for pies. Take care when separating the egg whites and yolks because even the smallest trace of yolk will prevent the whites from being whisked to their maximum volume. All equipment must be clean and free of grease.

1 Put the egg whites in a large, clean and grease-free bowl. With a whisk or electric mixer, whisk the whites until they are foamy.

2 Continue whisking until the whites hold soft peaks when you lift the whisk or beaters (the tips of the peaks will flop over).

SEPARATING EGGS

It is easier to separate the yolks and whites if eggs are cold. Tap the egg once or twice against the rim of a small bowl to crack the shell. Break open the shell and hold half in each hand. Carefully transfer the unbroken yolk from one half shell to the other several times, letting the egg white dribble into the bowl. Put the yolk in a second bowl.

4 Separate eggs carefully, making sure that there is no trace of egg yolk in the whites. (It is best to separate 1 egg at a time and check each white before adding it to the rest.)

3 Sprinkle over 50g/2oz/4 tbsp caster sugar for each egg white, whisking constantly. Continue whisking for about 1 minute or until the meringue is glossy and holds stiff peaks when you lift the whisk or beaters. The meringue is now ready to use.

--- COOK'S TIP ---

Egg whites can be whisked to their greatest volume if they are at room temperature rather than cold. A copper bowl and wire balloon whisk are the best tools to use, although a stainless steel or glass bowl and electric mixer also produce very good results.

PASTRY TIPS AND TECHNIQUES

ROLLING OUT AND LINING A TIN

A neat pastry case that doesn't distort or shrink in baking is the desired result. The key to success is handling the dough gently. Use the method here for lining a round pie or tart tin that is about 5cm/2in deep.

Remove the chilled dough from the refrigerator and allow it to soften slightly at room temperature. Unwrap and put it on a lightly floured surface. Flatten the dough into a neat round. Lightly flour the rolling pin.

1 Using even pressure, start rolling out the dough, working from the centre to the edge each time and easing the pressure slightly as you reach the edge of the round.

2 Lift up the dough and give it a quarter turn from time to time during the rolling. This will prevent the dough sticking to the surface and will help keep the thickness even.

3 Continue rolling out until the dough round is about 5cm/2in larger all round than the tin. The dough should be about 3mm/⅛in thick.

4 Set the rolling pin on the dough, near one side of the round. Fold the outside edge of the dough over the pin, then roll the rolling pin over the dough to wrap the dough around it. Do this gently and loosely.

5 Hold the rolling pin over the tin and gently unroll the dough so it drapes into the tin, centring it as much as possible.

6 With your fingertips, lift and ease the dough into the tin, gently pressing it over the bottom and up the side. Turn excess dough over the rim and trim it with a knife or scissors, depending on the edge to be made.

COOK'S TIPS

● Reflour the surface and rolling pin if the dough starts to stick.
● Should the dough tear, patch with a piece of moistened dough.
● When rolling out and lining the pie or tart tin, do not stretch the dough. It will only shrink back during baking, spoiling the shape of the pastry case.
● During rolling out, gently push in the edges of the dough with your cupped palms, to keep the round shape.

● A pastry scraper will help lift the dough from the work surface, to wrap it around the rolling pin.
● When finishing the edge, be sure to hook the dough over the rim all the way round or to press the dough firmly to the rim. This will prevent the dough pulling away should it start to shrink.
● Pie plates made from heat-resistant glass or dull-finish metal such as heavy-weight aluminium will give a crisp crust.

MAKING A PASTRY CASE

1 **For a forked edge**: trim the dough even with the rim and press it flat. Firmly and evenly press the prongs of a fork all round the edge. If the fork sticks, dip it in flour.

2 **For a crimped edge**: trim the dough to leave an overhang of about 1cm/½in all around. Fold the extra dough under. Use the knuckle or tip of the index finger of one of your hands and the thumb and index finger of your other hand to pinch the dough edge around your index finger into a 'V' shape. Continue all round the edge.

3 **For a cut-out edge**: trim the dough even with the rim and press it flat on the rim. With a small pastry cutter, cut out decorative shapes from the dough trimmings. Moisten the edge of the pastry case and press the cut-outs in place, overlapping them slightly if you like.

MAKING A TWO-CRUST PIE

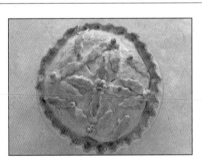

AMERICAN-STYLE APPLE PIE

1 Roll out half of the pastry dough on a floured surface and line a pie tin. Trim the edge. Add the apple filling and brush edge with water.

3 Trim the edge of the lid to leave a 1cm/½in overhang. Cut slits or a design in the centre. These will act as steam vents during baking.

2 Roll out a second piece of dough to a circle that is about 2.5cm/1in larger all round than the tin. Roll it up around the rolling pin and unroll over the pie. Press the edges together.

--- VARIATIONS ---

If covering a pie dish, roll the dough to a round or oval 5cm/2in larger than the dish. Cut a 2.5cm/1in strip from the outside and lay this on the moistened rim of the dish. Brush the strip with water and lay the sheet of dough on top. Press edges to seal, then trim even with the rim. Knock up the edge with a knife.

Combine 900g/2lb peeled, cored and thinly sliced Granny Smith apples, 15ml/1 tbsp plain flour, 90g/3½oz caster sugar and 2.5ml/½ tsp mixed spice. Toss to coat the fruit evenly with the sugar and flour. Use to fill the two-crust pie. Bake in a 190°C/375°F/Gas 5 oven for about 45 minutes or until the pastry is golden brown and the fruit is tender (test with a skewer through a slit in the top crust). Cool on a rack.

HOT PUDDINGS

On chilly days few things are more appealing than a warming pudding and there are recipes here for every occasion. Family favourites include Queen of Puddings, and Apple Brown Betty, but if you're looking for a new enticing idea, try the quick and tasty Thai Fried Bananas. For special occasions, the elegant Amaretto Soufflé is easier than you might imagine, and Warm Lemon and Syrup Cake, served with poached pears would make a delectable finale to a winter supper party.

Cinnamon and Coconut Rice

INGREDIENTS

Serves 4–6

40g/1½oz/¼ cup raisins
475ml/16fl oz/2 cups water
225g/8oz/1 cup short grain rice
1 cinnamon stick
25g/1oz/2 tbsp caster sugar
475ml/16fl oz/2 cups milk
250ml/8fl oz/1 cup canned sweetened
   coconut milk
2.5ml/½ tsp vanilla essence
15ml/1 tbsp butter
25g/1oz/⅓ cup desiccated coconut
ground cinnamon, for sprinkling

1 Soak the raisins in a small bowl in enough water to cover.

2 Bring the water to the boil in a medium-sized saucepan. Stir in the rice, cinnamon stick and sugar. Return to the boil, then lower the heat, cover, and simmer gently for 15–20 minutes, until the liquid is absorbed.

3 Meanwhile, blend the milk, coconut milk and vanilla essence together in a bowl. Drain the raisins.

4 Remove the cinnamon stick from the pan of rice. Add the raisins and the milk and coconut mixture and stir to mix. Continue cooking the rice, covered and stirring often, for about 20 minutes, until the mixture is just thick. Do not overcook the rice.

5 Preheat the grill. Transfer the rice to a flameproof serving dish. Dot with the butter and sprinkle with coconut. Grill about 13cm/5in from the heat for about 3–5 minutes, until just browned. Sprinkle with cinnamon. Serve warm, or cold, with cream if you like.

Queen of Puddings

This hot pudding was developed from a seventeenth-century recipe by Queen Victoria's chefs at Buckingham Palace and named in her honour.

INGREDIENTS

Serves 4

75g/3oz/1½ cups fresh breadcrumbs
60ml/4 tbsp caster sugar,
    plus 5ml/1 tsp
grated rind of 1 lemon
600ml/1 pint/2½ cups milk
4 eggs
45ml/3 tbsp raspberry jam, warmed

1 Stir the breadcrumbs, 30ml/2 tbsp of the sugar and the lemon rind together in a bowl. Bring the milk to the boil in a saucepan, then stir into the breadcrumbs.

2 Separate three of the eggs and beat the yolks with the whole egg. Stir into the breadcrumb mixture, pour into a buttered baking dish and leave to stand for 30 minutes.

3 Meanwhile, preheat the oven to 160°C/325°F/Gas 3. Bake the pudding for 50–60 minutes, until set.

COOK'S TIP

The traditional recipe calls for raspberry jam, but you may like to ring the changes by replacing it with another flavoured jam, lemon curd, marmalade or fruit purée.

4 Whisk the egg whites in a large, clean bowl until stiff but not dry, then gradually whisk in the remaining 30ml/2 tbsp caster sugar until the mixture is thick and glossy, taking care not to overwhip.

5 Spread the jam over the pudding, then spoon over the meringue to cover the top completely. Sprinkle the remaining sugar over the meringue, then bake for a further 15 minutes, until the meringue is beginning to turn a light golden colour.

Cabinet Pudding

INGREDIENTS

Serves 4

25g/1oz/2½ tbsp raisins, chopped
30ml/2 tbsp brandy (optional)
25g/1oz/2½ tbsp glacé cherries,
  halved
25g/1oz/2½ tbsp angelica, chopped
2 trifle sponge cakes, diced
50g/2oz ratafias, crushed
2 eggs
2 egg yolks
30ml/2 tbsp sugar
450ml/¾ pint/1⅞ cups single
  cream or milk
few drops of vanilla essence

COOK'S TIP

The pudding can be cooked in an ordinary baking dish, if preferred, and served from the dish.

---

1 Soak the raisins in the brandy, if using, for several hours.

2 Butter a 750ml/1¼ pint/3⅔ cup charlotte mould and arrange some of the cherries and angelica in the base.

3 Mix the remaining cherries and angelica with the sponge cakes, ratafias and raisins and brandy, if using, and spoon into the mould.

4 Lightly whisk together the eggs, egg yolks and sugar. Bring the cream or milk just to the boil, then stir into the egg mixture with the vanilla essence.

5 Strain the egg mixture into the mould, then leave for 15–30 minutes.

6 Preheat the oven to 160°C/325°F/ Gas 3. Place the mould in a roasting tin, cover with baking paper and pour in boiling water. Bake for 1 hour, or until set. Leave for 2–3 minutes, then turn out on to a warm plate.

Eve's Pudding

The tempting apples beneath the sponge topping are the reason for the pudding's name.

INGREDIENTS

Serves 4–6

115g/4oz/½ cup butter
115g/4oz/½ cup caster sugar
2 eggs, beaten
grated rind and juice of 1 lemon
90g/3½oz/scant 1cup self-raising
  flour
40g/1½oz/⅓ cup ground almonds
115g/4oz/scant ½ cup soft brown
  sugar
500–675g/1½lb cooking apples, cored
  and thinly sliced
25g/1oz/¼ cup flaked almonds

1 Beat together the butter and caster sugar in a large mixing bowl until the mixture is very light and fluffy.

2 Gradually beat the eggs into the butter mixture, beating well after each addition, then fold in the lemon rind, flour and ground almonds.

3 Mix the brown sugar, apples and lemon juice, tip into the dish, add the sponge mixture, then the almonds. Bake for 40–45 minutes, until golden.

Apple Brown Betty

INGREDIENTS

Serves 6

50g/2oz/1 cup fresh white breadcrumbs
175g/6oz/¾ cup soft light brown sugar
2.5ml/½ tsp ground cinnamon
1.25ml/¼ tsp ground cloves
1.25ml/¼ tsp grated nutmeg
50g/2oz/4 tbsp butter
1kg/2lb cooking apples
juice of 1 lemon
25g/1oz/⅓ cup finely chopped walnuts
cream or ice cream, to serve

1 Preheat the grill. Spread out the breadcrumbs on a baking sheet and toast under the grill until golden, stirring frequently to colour them evenly. Set aside. Preheat the oven to 190°C/375°F/Gas 5. Butter a large deep ovenproof dish.

2 Mix the sugar with the cinnamon, cloves and nutmeg. Cut the butter into tiny pieces, then set aside.

3 Peel, core, and slice the apples. Toss immediately with the lemon juice to prevent the apple slices from turning brown.

4 Sprinkle 30–45ml/2–3 tbsp of the breadcrumbs into the prepared dish. Cover with one-third of the apples and sprinkle with one-third of the sugar and spice mixture. Add another layer of breadcrumbs and dot with one-third of the butter. Repeat the layers two more times, ending with a layer of breadcrumbs. Sprinkle with the nuts, and dot with the remaining butter.

5 Bake for 35–40 minutes, until the apples are tender and the top is golden brown. Serve warm with cream or ice cream, if you like.

Creole Bread and Butter Pudding

INGREDIENTS

Serves 4–6

4 ready-to-eat dried apricots, chopped
15ml/1 tbsp raisins
30ml/2 tbsp sultanas
15ml/1 tbsp chopped mixed peel
1 French loaf (about 200g/7oz), thinly
 sliced
50g/2oz/4 tbsp butter, melted
450ml/¾ pint/1⅞ cups milk
150ml/¼ pint/⅔ cup double cream
115g/4oz/½ cup caster sugar
3 eggs
2.5ml/½ tsp vanilla essence
30ml/2 tbsp whisky

For the cream

150ml/¼ pint/⅔ cup double cream
30ml/2 tbsp Greek-style yogurt
15–30ml/1–2 tbsp whisky
15ml/1 tbsp caster sugar

1 Preheat the oven to 180°C/350°F/
Gas 4. Lightly grease a deep
1.5–1.75 litre/2½ pint/6 cup ovenproof
dish with butter. Mix together the dried
fruits and sprinkle a little over the base
of the dish. Brush both sides of the
bread slices with melted butter.

2 Fill the dish with alternate layers of
bread slices and dried fruit, finishing with a layer of bread.

3 Heat the milk and cream together in
a pan until just boiling. Meanwhile,
place the sugar, eggs and vanilla essence
in a bowl and whisk together.

4 Whisk the hot milk and cream into
the eggs and then strain over the
bread and fruit. Sprinkle the whisky
over the top. Press the bread into the
milk and egg mixture, cover with foil
and leave to stand for 20 minutes.

5 Place the dish in a roasting tin half-
filled with water and bake for about
1 hour or until the custard is just set.
Remove the foil and return the pudding
to the oven to cook for a further 10
minutes, until the bread is golden.

6 Just before serving, place the cream,
Greek yogurt, whisky and sugar
into a small pan, stir and heat gently.
Serve with the hot pudding.

Crêpes Suzette

INGREDIENTS

Makes 8

115g/4oz/1 cup plain flour
pinch of salt
1 egg
1 egg yolk
300ml/½ pint/1¼ cups semi-skimmed milk
15g/½oz/1 tbsp butter, melted, plus extra for frying

For the sauce

2 large oranges
50g/2oz/4 tbsp butter
50g/2oz/½ cup soft light brown sugar
15ml/1 tbsp Grand Marnier
15ml/1 tbsp brandy

1 Sift the flour and salt into a bowl and make a well in the centre. Crack the egg and extra yolk into the well.

2 Stir the eggs with a wooden spoon to incorporate the flour from round the edges. When the mixture thickens, gradually pour on the milk, beating well after each addition, until a smooth batter is formed.

3 Stir in the butter, transfer to a jug, cover and chill for 30 minutes.

4 Heat a medium (about 20cm/8in) shallow frying pan, add a little butter and heat until sizzling. Pour on a little of the batter, tilting the pan back and forth to cover the base thinly.

5 Cook over a medium heat for 1–2 minutes until lightly browned underneath, then flip over using a palette knife and cook for a further minute. Repeat this process until you have eight crêpes. Stack them up on a plate, as they are ready.

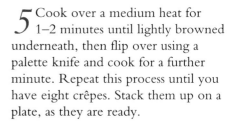

6 Using a zester, pare the rind from one of the oranges and reserve about a teaspoon for decoration. Squeeze the juice from both oranges and set aside.

7 To make the sauce, melt the butter in a large frying pan and add the sugar with the orange rind and juice. Heat gently until the sugar has just dissolved and the mixture is gently bubbling. Fold each crêpe in quarters. Add to the pan one at a time, coating in the sauce and folding each one in half again. Gently move to the side of the pan to make room for the others.

8 Pour on the Grand Marnier and brandy and cook gently for 2–3 minutes, until the sauce has slightly caramelized. (For that extra touch, flame the brandy as you pour it into the pan.) Sprinkle with the reserved orange rind and serve straight from the pan.

Surprise Lemon Pudding

The surprise is a delicious, tangy lemon sauce that forms beneath the light topping.

INGREDIENTS

Serves 4

75g/3oz/6 tbsp butter
175g/6oz/⅔ cup soft brown sugar
4 eggs, separated
grated rind and juice of 4 lemons
50g/2oz/½ cup self-raising flour
120ml/4fl oz/½ cup milk

1 Preheat the oven to 180°C/350°F/ Gas 4. Butter an 18cm/7in soufflé dish or deep cake tin and stand it in a roasting tin.

2 Beat the butter and sugar together in a large bowl until pale and very fluffy. Beat in 1 egg yolk at a time, beating well after each addition and gradually beating in the lemon rind and juice until well mixed; do not worry if the mixture curdles a little.

3 Sift the flour and stir into the lemon mixture until well mixed, then gradually stir in the milk.

4 Whisk the egg whites in a separate bowl until stiff but not dry, then lightly, but thoroughly, fold into the lemon mixture in three batches. Carefully pour the mixture into the soufflé dish or cake tin, then pour boiling water around.

5 Bake the pudding in the middle of the oven for about 45 minutes, or until risen, just firm to the touch and golden brown on top. Serve at once.

Spiced Mexican Fritters

Hot, sweet and spicy fritters are popular in both Spain and Mexico for either breakfast or a mid-morning snack.

INGREDIENTS

Makes 16 (serves 4)
175g/6oz/1¼ cups raspberries
45ml/3 tbsp icing sugar
45ml/3 tbsp orange juice

For the fritters
50g/2oz/4 tbsp butter
65g/2½oz/⅔ cup plain flour, sifted
2 eggs, lightly beaten
15ml/1 tbsp ground almonds
corn oil, for frying
15ml/1 tbsp icing sugar and 2.5ml/
  ½ tsp ground cinnamon, for dusting
8 fresh raspberries, to decorate

1 First make the raspberry sauce. Mash the raspberries with the icing sugar and then push through a sieve into a bowl to remove all the seeds. Stir in the orange juice and chill while making the fritters.

2 To make the fritters, place the butter and 150ml/¼ pint/⅔ cup water in a saucepan and heat gently until the butter has melted. Bring to the boil and, when boiling, add the sifted flour all at once and turn off the heat.

3 Beat until the mixture leaves the sides of the pan and forms a ball. Cool slightly then beat in the eggs a little at a time, then add the almonds.

4 Spoon the mixture into a piping bag fitted with a large star nozzle. Half-fill a saucepan or deep-fat fryer with the oil and heat to 190°C/375°F.

5 Pipe about four 5cm/2in lengths at a time into the hot oil, cutting off the raw mixture with a knife as you go. Deep-fry for about 3–4 minutes, turning occasionally, until puffed up and golden. Drain on kitchen paper and keep warm in the oven while frying the remainder.

6 When you have fried all the mixture, dust the hot fritters with icing sugar and cinnamon. Serve three or four per person on serving plates drizzled with a little of the raspberry sauce, dust again with sieved icing sugar and decorate with fresh raspberries.

Thai Fried Bananas

A very simple and quick Thai pudding – bananas fried in butter, brown sugar and lime juice, and sprinkled with toasted coconut.

INGREDIENTS

Serves 4
40g/1½oz/3 tbsp butter
4 large slightly underripe bananas
15ml/1 tbsp desiccated coconut
60ml/4 tbsp soft light brown sugar
60ml/4 tbsp lime juice
2 fresh lime slices, to decorate
thick and creamy natural yogurt,
  to serve

1 Heat the butter in a large frying pan or wok and fry the bananas for 1–2 minutes on each side, or until they are lightly golden in colour.

2 Meanwhile, dry-fry the coconut in a small frying pan until lightly browned, and reserve.

3 Sprinkle the sugar into the pan with the bananas, add the lime juice and cook, stirring until dissolved. Sprinkle the coconut over the bananas, decorate with lime slices and serve with the thick and creamy yogurt.

Amaretto Soufflé

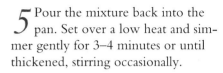

INGREDIENTS

Serves 6

6 amaretti biscuits, coarsely crushed
90ml/6 tbsp Amaretto liqueur
4 eggs, separated, plus 1 egg white
105ml/7 tbsp caster sugar
30ml/2 tbsp plain flour
250ml/8fl oz/1 cup milk
pinch of cream of tartar (if needed)
icing sugar, for dusting

1 Preheat the oven to 200°C/400°F/ Gas 6. Butter a 1.5 litre/2½ pint soufflé dish and sprinkle it with a little of the caster sugar.

2 Put the biscuits in a bowl. Sprinkle them with 30ml/2 tbsp of the Amaretto liqueur and set aside.

3 Mix together the 4 egg yolks, 30ml/2 tbsp of the sugar and flour.

4 Heat the milk just to the boil in a heavy saucepan. Gradually add the hot milk to the egg mixture, stirring.

5 Pour the mixture back into the pan. Set over a low heat and simmer gently for 3–4 minutes or until thickened, stirring occasionally.

6 Add the remaining Amaretto liqueur. Remove from the heat.

7 In a scrupulously clean, grease-free bowl, whisk the 5 egg whites until they will hold soft peaks. (If not using a copper bowl, add the cream of tartar as soon as the whites are frothy.) Add the remaining sugar and continue whisking until stiff.

8 Add about one-quarter of the whites to the liqueur mixture and stir in with a rubber spatula. Add the remaining whites and fold in gently.

9 Spoon half of the mixture into the prepared soufflé dish. Cover with a layer of the moistened amaretti biscuits, then spoon the remaining soufflé mixture on top.

10 Bake for 20 minutes or until the soufflé is risen and lightly browned. Sprinkle with sifted icing sugar and serve immediately.

> — COOK'S TIP —
>
> Some people like soufflés to be completely cooked. Others prefer a soft, creamy centre. The choice is up to you. To check how cooked the middle is, insert a thin skewer into the centre: it will come out almost clean or with some moist particles clinging to it.

Warm Lemon and Syrup Cake

INGREDIENTS

Serves 8

3 eggs
175g/6oz/¾ cup butter, softened
175g/6oz/¾ cup caster sugar
175g/6oz/1½ cups self-raising flour
50g/2oz/½ cup ground almonds
1.25ml/¼ tsp freshly grated nutmeg
50g/2oz candied lemon peel,
    finely chopped
grated rind of 1 lemon
30ml/2 tbsp lemon juice
poached pears, to serve

For the syrup

175g/6oz/¾ cup caster sugar
juice of 3 lemons

1 Preheat the oven to 180°C/350°F/
Gas 4. Grease and base-line a deep,
round 20cm/8in cake tin.

2 Place all the cake ingredients in a
large bowl and beat well for 2–3
minutes, until light and fluffy.

3 Tip the mixture into the prepared
tin, spread level and bake for 1 hour,
or until golden and firm to the touch.

4 Meanwhile, make the syrup. Put
the sugar, lemon juice and 75ml/5
tbsp water in a pan. Heat gently, stirring
until the sugar has dissolved, then boil,
without stirring, for 1–2 minutes.

5 Turn out the cake on to a plate with
a rim. Prick the surface of the cake
all over with a fork, then pour over the
hot syrup. Leave to soak for about 30
minutes. Serve the cake warm with thin
wedges of poached pears.

Apple Strudel

This Austrian pudding is traditionally made with paper-thin layers of buttered strudel pastry, filled with spiced apples and nuts. Ready-made filo pastry makes an easy substitute.

INGREDIENTS

Serves 4–6
75g/3oz/¾ cup hazelnuts, chopped
  and roasted
30ml/2 tbsp nibbed almonds, roasted
50g/2oz/4 tbsp demerara sugar
2.5ml/½ tsp ground cinnamon
grated rind and juice of ½ lemon
2 large Bramley cooking apples,
  peeled, cored and chopped
50g/2oz/⅓ cup sultanas
4 large sheets filo pastry
50g/2oz/4 tbsp unsalted butter, melted
icing sugar, for dusting
cream, custard or yogurt, to serve

1 Preheat the oven to 190°C/375°F/ Gas 5. In a bowl mix together the hazelnuts, almonds, sugar, cinnamon, lemon rind and juice, apples and sultanas. Set aside.

2 Lay one sheet of filo pastry on a clean dish towel and brush with melted butter. Lay a second sheet on top and brush again with melted butter. Repeat with the remaining two sheets.

3 Spread the fruit and nut mixture over the pastry, leaving a 7.5cm/3in border at each of the shorter ends. Fold the pastry ends in over the filling. Roll up from one long edge to the other, using the dish towel to help.

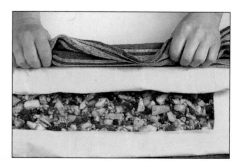

4 Carefully transfer the strudel to a greased baking sheet, placing the seam side down. Brush all over with butter and bake for 30–35 minutes, until golden and crisp. Dust with icing sugar and serve while still hot with cream, custard or yogurt.

Chocolate Fruit Fondue

Fondues originated in Switzerland and this sweet treat is the perfect ending to any meal.

INGREDIENTS

Serves 6–8
16 fresh strawberries
4 rings fresh pineapple, cut into wedges
2 small nectarines, stoned and cut into
  wedges
1 kiwi fruit, halved and thickly sliced
small bunch of black seedless grapes
2 bananas, chopped
1 small eating apple, cored and cut into
  wedges
lemon juice, for brushing
225g/8oz plain chocolate
15g/½oz/1 tbsp butter
150ml/¼ pint/⅔ cup single cream
45ml/3 tbsp Irish cream liqueur
15ml/1 tbsp pistachio nuts, chopped

1 Arrange the fruit on a serving platter and brush the banana and apple pieces with a little lemon juice. Cover and chill until ready to serve.

2 Place the chocolate, butter, cream and liqueur in a heatproof bowl over a pan of gently simmering water. Stir occasionally until melted and completely smooth.

3 Pour the chocolate mixture into a warmed serving bowl and sprinkle with the pistachios. To serve, guests help themselves by skewering fruits on to fondue forks or dessert forks and dipping in the hot chocolate sauce.

COLD DESSERTS

Chilled desserts are perfect to make when you are entertaining and there are classic dinner party dishes here, such as Australian Hazelnut Pavlova, Summer Pudding, and Peach Melba, as well as some innovative variations on old ideas that are sure to impress. Try the light, tangy cheesecake served in individual slices atop brandy snaps, or the glittering, dark coffee jellies. But that's not all; there are everyday desserts, too, and Apricot Mousse, and Rhubarb and Orange Fool are just as delicious to eat.

Gooseberry and Elderflower Cream

When elderflowers are in season, instead of using the cordial, cook two to three elderflower heads with the gooseberries.

INGREDIENTS

Serves 4

500g/1¼lb gooseberries, topped and
   tailed
300ml/½ pint/1¼ cups double cream
about 115g/4oz/1 cup icing
   sugar, to taste
30ml/2 tbsp elderflower cordial or
   orange flower water (optional)
mint sprigs, to decorate
almond biscuits, to serve

1 Place the gooseberries in a heavy saucepan, cover and cook over a low heat, shaking the pan occasionally, until the gooseberries are tender. Tip the gooseberries into a bowl, crush them, then leave to cool completely.

2 Beat the cream until soft peaks form, then fold in half the crushed gooseberries. Sweeten and add elderflower cordial, or orange flower water to taste, if using. Sweeten the remaining gooseberries.

3 Layer the cream mixture and the crushed gooseberries in four dessert dishes or tall glasses, then cover and chill. Decorate with mint sprigs and serve with almond biscuits.

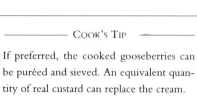

COOK'S TIP

If preferred, the cooked gooseberries can be puréed and sieved. An equivalent quantity of real custard can replace the cream.

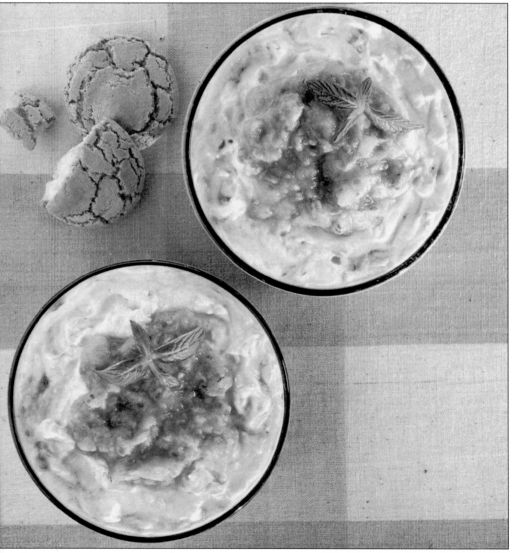

Honeycomb Mould

These delectable desserts have a fresh, clear lemon flavour. They look attractive when unmoulded, as the mixture sets in layers.

INGREDIENTS

Serves 4

30ml/2 tbsp cold water
15g/½oz/1 sachet powdered
  gelatine
2 eggs, separated
75g/3oz/scant ½ cup caster sugar
475ml/16fl oz/2 cups milk
grated rind of 1 small lemon
60ml/4 tbsp freshly squeezed
  lemon juice

1 Chill four individual moulds, or a 1.2 litre/2 pint/5 cup jelly mould.

2 Pour the water into a small bowl, sprinkle over the gelatine and leave to soften for 5 minutes. Place the bowl over a small saucepan of hot water and stir occasionally until dissolved.

3 Meanwhile, whisk the egg yolks and sugar together until pale, thick and fluffy.

4 Bring the milk to the boil in a heavy, preferably non-stick, saucepan, then slowly pour on to the egg yolks, stirring.

5 Return the milk mixture to the pan then heat gently, stirring, until thickened; do not allow to boil. Remove from the heat and stir in the lemon rind and juice.

6 Stir 2 or 3 spoonfuls of the lemon mixture into the gelatine, then stir back into the saucepan. In a clean dry bowl, whisk the egg whites until stiff but not dry, then gently fold into the mixture in the pan in three batches.

7 Rinse the moulds or mould with cold water and drain well, then pour in the lemon mixture. Leave to cool, then cover and chill until set and ready to unmould and serve.

Raspberry and Honey Cream

INGREDIENTS

Serves 4

60ml/4 tbsp clear honey
45ml/3 tbsp whisky
50g/2oz/⅔ cup medium oatmeal
300ml/½ pint/1¼ cups double cream
350g/12oz raspberries
mint sprigs, to decorate

1 Gently warm the honey in the whisky, then leave to cool.

2 Preheat the grill. Spread the oatmeal in a very shallow layer in the grill pan and toast, stirring occasionally, until browned. Leave to cool.

3 Whip the cream in a large bowl until soft peaks form, then gently stir in the oats, honey and whisky until well combined.

4 Reserve a few raspberries for decoration, then layer the remainder with the oat mixture in four tall glasses. Cover and chill for 2 hours.

5 About 30 minutes before serving, transfer the glasses to room temperature. Decorate with the reserved raspberries and mint sprigs.

Summer Fruit Trifle

INGREDIENTS

Serves 6

75g/3oz day-old sponge cake, broken into bite-size pieces
8 ratafias, broken into halves
100ml/3½fl oz/⅓ cup medium sherry
30ml/2 tbsp brandy
350g/12oz prepared fruit such as raspberries, strawberries or peaches
300ml/½ pint/1¼ cups double cream
40g/1½oz/⅓ cup toasted flaked almonds
strawberries, to decorate

For the custard

4 egg yolks
25g/1oz/2 tbsp caster sugar
450ml/¾ pint/scant 2 cups single or whipping cream
few drops of vanilla essence

1 Put the sponge cake and ratafias in a glass serving dish, then sprinkle over the sherry and brandy and leave until they have been absorbed.

2 To make the custard, whisk the egg yolks and sugar together. Bring the cream to the boil in a heavy saucepan, then pour on to the egg yolk mixture, stirring constantly.

3 Return the mixture to the pan and heat very gently, stirring all the time with a wooden spoon, until the custard thickens enough to coat the back of the spoon; do not allow to boil. Leave to cool, stirring occasionally.

4 Put the fruit in an even layer over the sponge cake in the serving dish, then strain the custard over the fruit and leave to set. Lightly whip the cream, spread it over the custard, then chill the trifle well. Decorate with flaked almonds and strawberries just before serving.

Chocolate Blancmange

For a special dinner party, flavour the blancmange with peppermint essence, crème de menthe or orange liqueur, and decorate with whipped cream and white and plain chocolate curls.

INGREDIENTS

Serves 4
60ml/4 tbsp cornflour
600ml/1 pint/2½ cups milk
45ml/3 tbsp sugar
50–115g/2–4 oz plain chocolate, chopped
few drops vanilla essence
chocolate curls, to decorate

1 Rinse a 750ml/1¼ pint/3 cup fluted mould with cold water and leave it upside-down to drain. Blend the cornflour to a smooth paste with a little of the milk.

2 Bring the remaining milk to the boil, preferably in a non-stick saucepan, then pour on to the blended mixture stirring all the time.

3 Pour all the milk back into the saucepan and bring slowly to the boil over a low heat, stirring all the time until the mixture boils and thickens. Remove the pan from the heat, then add the sugar, chopped chocolate and vanilla essence and stir until the sauce is smooth and the chocolate melted.

4 Pour the chocolate mixture into the mould and leave in a cool place for several hours to set.

5 To unmould the blancmange, place a large serving plate over the mould, then holding the plate and mould firmly together, invert them. Give both plate and mould a gentle but firm shake to loosen the blancmange, then lift off the mould. Scatter the white and plain chocolate curls over the top of the blancmange and serve at once.

COOK'S TIP

If you prefer, set the blancmange in four or six individual moulds.

Australian Hazelnut Pavlova

INGREDIENTS

Serves 4–6

3 egg whites
175g/6oz/¾ cup caster sugar
5ml/1 tsp cornflour
5ml/1 tsp white wine vinegar
40g/1½oz/5 tbsp chopped roasted
    hazelnuts
250ml/8fl oz/1 cup double cream
15ml/1 tbsp orange juice
30ml/2 tbsp natural thick and creamy
    yogurt
2 ripe nectarines, stoned and sliced
225g/8oz/2 cups raspberries, halved
15–30ml/1–2 tbsp redcurrant jelly,
    warmed

1 Preheat the oven to 140°C/275°F/
Gas 1. Lightly grease a baking sheet.
Draw a 20cm/8in circle on a sheet of
baking parchment. Place pencil-side
down on the baking sheet.

2 Place the egg whites in a clean,
grease-free bowl and whisk with an
electric mixer until stiff. Whisk in the
sugar 15ml/1 tbsp at a time, whisking
well after each addition.

3 Add the cornflour, vinegar and
hazelnuts and fold in carefully with
a large metal spoon.

4 Spoon the meringue on to the
marked circle and spread out to the
edges, making a dip in the centre.

5 Bake for about 1¼–1½ hours, until
crisp. Leave to cool completely
and transfer to a serving platter.

6 Whip the cream and orange juice
until just thick, stir in the yogurt
and spoon on to the meringue. Top
with the fruit and drizzle over the redcurrant jelly. Serve immediately.

Peach Melba

The original dish created for the opera singer Dame Nellie Melba had peaches and ice cream served upon an ice swan.

INGREDIENTS

Serves 4
300g/11oz raspberries
squeeze of lemon juice
icing sugar, to taste
2 large ripe peaches or 1 x 425g/15oz
    can sliced peaches
8 scoops vanilla ice cream

1 Press the raspberries through a non-metallic sieve.

2 Add a little lemon juice to the raspberry purée and sweeten to taste with icing sugar.

3 Dip fresh peaches in boiling water for 4–5 seconds, then slip off the skins, halve along the indented line, then slice, or tip canned peaches into a sieve and drain.

4 Place two scoops of ice cream in each individual glass dish, top with peach slices, then pour over the raspberry purée. Serve immediately.

> — COOK'S TIP —
>
> If you'd like to prepare this ahead, scoop the ice cream on to a cold baking sheet and freeze until ready to serve, then transfer the scoops to the dishes.

Summer Pudding

INGREDIENTS

Serves 4
about 8 thin slices day-old white
    bread, crusts removed
800g/1¾lb mixed summer fruits
about 30ml/2 tbsp sugar

1 Cut a round from one slice of bread to fit in the base of a 1.2 litre/ 2 pint/5 cup pudding basin, then cut strips of bread about 5cm/2in wide to line the basin, overlapping the strips.

2 Gently heat the fruit, sugar and 30ml/2 tbsp water in a large heavy saucepan, shaking the pan occasionally, until the juices begin to run.

3 Reserve about 45ml/3 tbsp fruit juice, then spoon the fruit and remaining juice into the basin, taking care not to dislodge the bread.

4 Cut the remaining bread to fit entirely over the fruit. Stand the basin on a plate and cover with a saucer or small plate that will just fit inside the top of the basin. Place a heavy weight on top. Chill the pudding and the reserved fruit juice overnight.

5 Run a knife carefully around the inside of the basin rim, then invert the pudding on to a cold serving plate. Pour over the reserved juice and serve.

Eton Mess

This dish forms part of the picnic meals parents and pupils enjoy on the lawns at Eton College's annual prize-giving in early June.

INGREDIENTS

Serves 4

500g/1¼lb strawberries, chopped
45–60ml/3–4 tbsp Kirsch
300ml/½ pint/1¼ cups double cream
6 small white meringues
mint sprigs, to decorate

1 Put the strawberries in a bowl, sprinkle over the Kirsch, then cover and chill for 2–3 hours.

2 Whip the cream until soft peaks form, then gently fold in the strawberries with their juices.

3 Crush the meringues into rough chunks, then scatter over the strawberry mixture and fold in gently.

4 Spoon the strawberry mixture into a glass serving bowl, decorate with mint sprigs and serve immediately.

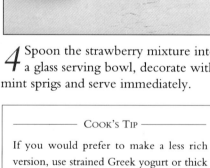

COOK'S TIP

If you would prefer to make a less rich version, use strained Greek yogurt or thick natural yogurt instead of part or all of the cream. Simply beat the yogurt gently before adding the strawberries.

Lemon Cheesecake on Brandy Snaps

Cheating with ready-made brandy snaps gives a quick and crunchy golden base to a simple classic cheesecake mixture.

INGREDIENTS

Serves 8
½ x 142g/4¾oz packet lemon jelly
450g/1lb/2 cups low fat cream cheese
10ml/2 tsp lemon rind
75–115g/3–4oz/about ½ cup caster
    sugar
few drops vanilla essence
150ml/¼ pint/⅔ cup Greek-style
    yogurt
8 brandy snaps
mint leaves and icing sugar, to decorate

1 Dissolve the jelly in 45–60ml/3–4 tbsp boiling water in a heatproof measuring jug and, when clear, add sufficient cold water to make up to 150ml/¼ pint/⅔ cup. Chill until beginning to thicken. Line a 450g/1lb loaf tin with clear film.

2 Cream the cheese with the lemon rind, sugar and vanilla and beat until light and smooth. Then fold in the thickening lemon jelly and the yogurt. Spoon into the prepared tin and chill until set. Preheat the oven to 160°C/325°F/Gas 3.

3 Place two or three brandy snaps at a time on a baking sheet. Place in the oven for no more than 1 minute, until soft enough to unroll and flatten out completely. Leave on a cold plate or tray to harden again. Repeat with the remaining brandy snaps.

4 To serve, turn the cheesecake out on to a board with the help of the clear film. Cut into eight slices and place one slice on each brandy snap base. Decorate with mint leaves and sprinkle with icing sugar.

—————— COOK'S TIP ——————

If you don't have any brandy snaps to hand, you could serve this cheesecake on thin slices of moist ginger cake, or on other thin, crisp biscuits.

Coffee, Vanilla and Chocolate Stripe

INGREDIENTS

Serves 6

285g/10½oz/1½ cups caster sugar
90ml/6 tbsp cornflour
900ml/1½ pints/4 cups milk
3 egg yolks
75g/3oz/6 tbsp unsalted butter, at
 room temperature
20ml/generous 1 tbsp instant coffee
 powder
10ml/2 tsp vanilla essence
30ml/2 tbsp cocoa powder
whipped cream, to serve

3 Divide the coffee mixture among six wine glasses. Smooth the tops before the mixture sets.

4 Wipe any dribbles on the insides and outsides of the glasses with damp kitchen paper.

5 To make the vanilla layer, place half of the remaining sugar and cornflour in a heavy-based saucepan. Whisk in 300ml/½ pint/1⅓ cups of the milk. Over a medium heat, whisk in another egg yolk and bring to the boil, whisking. Boil for 1 minute.

6 Remove the pan from the heat and stir in 25g/1oz/2 tbsp of the butter and the vanilla. Leave to cool slightly, then spoon into the glasses on top of the coffee layer. Smooth the tops and wipe the glasses with kitchen paper.

1 To make the coffee layer, place 90g/3½oz/½ cup of the sugar and 30ml/2 tbsp of the cornflour in a heavy-based saucepan. Gradually add one-third of the milk, whisking until well blended. Over a medium heat, whisk in one of the egg yolks and bring to the boil, whisking. Boil for 1 minute.

2 Remove the pan from the heat. Stir in 25g/1oz/2 tbsp of the butter and the instant coffee powder. Set aside in the pan to cool slightly.

7 To make the chocolate layer, place the remaining sugar and cornflour in a heavy-based saucepan. Gradually whisk in the remaining milk and continue whisking until blended. Over a medium heat, whisk in the last egg yolk and bring to the boil, whisking constantly. Boil for 1 minute. Remove from the heat, stir in the remaining butter and the cocoa. Leave to cool slightly, then spoon into the glasses on top of the vanilla layer. Chill until set.

8 Pipe swirls of whipped cream on top of each dessert before serving.

COOK'S TIP

For a special occasion, prepare the vanilla layer using a fresh vanilla pod. Choose a plump, supple pod and split it down the centre with a sharp knife. Add to the mixture with the milk and discard the pod before spooning the mixture into the glasses. The flavour will be more pronounced and the pudding will have pretty brown speckles from the vanilla seeds.

Boodles Orange Fool

This fool became the speciality of Boodles Club, a gentlemen's club in London's St James's.

INGREDIENTS

Serves 4
4 trifle sponge cakes, cubed
300ml/½ pint/1¼ cups double
  cream
30–60ml/2–4 tbsp caster sugar
grated rind and juice of 2 oranges
grated rind and juice of 1 lemon
orange and lemon slices and rind,
  to decorate

1 Line the base and halfway up the sides of a large glass serving bowl or china dish with the cubed trifle sponge cakes.

2 Whip the cream with the sugar until it starts to thicken, then gradually whip in the fruit juices, adding the fruit rinds towards the end.

3 Carefully pour the cream mixture into the bowl or dish, taking care not to dislodge the sponge. Cover and chill for 3–4 hours. Serve decorated with orange and lemon slices and rind.

—— WATCHPOINT ——
Take care not to overwhip the cream mixture – it should just hold soft peaks.

Apricot and Orange Jelly

INGREDIENTS

Serves 4
350g/12oz well-flavoured fresh ripe
  apricots, stoned
50–75g/2–3oz/about ⅓ cup sugar
about 300ml/½ pint/1¼ cups freshly
  squeezed orange juice
15ml/1 tbsp powdered gelatine
single cream, to serve
finely chopped candied orange peel, to
  decorate

1 Heat the apricots, sugar and 120ml/4fl oz/½ cup orange juice, stirring until the sugar has dissolved. Simmer gently until the apricots are tender.

2 Press the apricot mixture through a nylon sieve into a small measuring jug using a spoon.

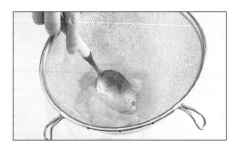

3 Pour 45ml/3 tbsp orange juice into a small heatproof bowl, sprinkle over the gelatine and leave for about 5 minutes, until softened.

4 Place the bowl over a saucepan of hot water and heat until the gelatine has dissolved. Slowly pour into the apricot mixture, stirring all the time. Make up to 600ml/1 pint/2½ cups with orange juice.

5 Pour the apricot mixture into four individual dishes and chill until set. Pour a thin layer of cream over the surface of the jellies before serving, decorated with candied orange peel.

Fruit and Rice Ring

This unusual rice pudding looks beautiful turned out of a ring mould but if you prefer, stir the fruit into the rice and serve in individual dishes.

INGREDIENTS 🍎

Serves 4

65g/2½oz/5 tbsp short grain rice
900ml/1½ pints/3¾ cups semi-
  skimmed milk
1 cinnamon stick
175g/6oz/1½ cups mixed dried fruit
175g/6fl oz/¾ cup orange juice
45ml/3 tbsp sugar
finely grated rind of 1 small orange

1 Place the rice, milk, and cinnamon stick in a large pan and bring to a boil. Cover and simmer, stirring occasionally, for about 1½ hours, until no liquid remains.

2 Meanwhile, place the fruit and orange juice in another pan and bring to the boil. Cover and simmer very gently for about 1 hour, until tender and no liquid remains.

3 Remove the cinnamon stick from the rice and stir in the sugar and orange rind.

4 Tip the fruit into the base of a lightly oiled 1.5 litre/2½ pint/ 6 cup ring mould. Spoon the rice over, smoothing down firmly. Chill.

5 Run a knife around the edge of the mould and turn out the rice carefully on to a serving plate.

Raspberry and Passion Fruit Swirls

If passion fruit is not available, this simple dessert can be made with raspberries alone.

INGREDIENTS 🍎

Serves 4
300g/11oz/2½ cups raspberries
2 passion fruit
400g/14oz/1⅔ cups low fat fromage
    frais
30ml/2 tbsp sugar
raspberries and sprigs of mint,
    to decorate

1 Mash the raspberries in a small bowl with a fork until the juice runs. Scoop out the passion fruit pulp into a separate bowl with the fromage frais and sugar and mix well.

2 Spoon alternate spoonfuls of the raspberry pulp and the fromage frais mixture into stemmed glasses or one large serving dish, stirring lightly to create a swirled effect.

3 Decorate each dessert with a whole raspberry and a sprig of fresh mint. Serve chilled.

— COOK'S TIP —

Over-ripe, slightly soft fruit can also be used in this recipe. You could use frozen raspberries when fresh are not available, but thaw them first.

— VARIATION —

Other summer fruits would be just as delicious – try a mix of strawberries and redcurrants with the raspberries, or use mangoes, peaches or apricots, which you will need to purée in a food processor or blender before mixing with the fromage frais.

Apricots with Orange Cream

Mascarpone is a very rich cream cheese made from thick Lombardy cream. It is delicious flavoured with orange as a topping for these poached, chilled apricots.

Ingredients

Serves 4

450g/1lb/2½ cups ready-to-eat dried
    apricots
strip of lemon peel
1 cinnamon stick
45ml/3 tbsp caster sugar
150ml/¼ pint/⅔ cup sweet dessert
    wine (such as Muscat de Beaumes de
    Venise)
115g/4oz/½ cup mascarpone cream
    cheese
45ml/3 tbsp orange juice
pinch of ground cinnamon and fresh
    mint sprig, to decorate

1 Place the apricots, lemon peel, cinnamon stick and 15ml/1 tbsp of the sugar in a pan and cover with 450ml/¾ pint/1⅞ cups cold water. Bring to the boil, cover and simmer gently for 25 minutes, until the fruit is tender.

2 Remove from the heat and stir in the dessert wine. Leave until cold, then chill for 3–4 hours or overnight.

3 Mix together the mascarpone cheese, orange juice and remaining sugar in a bowl and beat well until smooth. Chill until required.

4 Just before serving remove the cinnamon stick and lemon peel from the apricots and serve with a spoonful of the chilled mascarpone orange cream sprinkled with a little cinnamon and decorated with a sprig of fresh mint.

Rhubarb and Orange Fool

Perhaps this traditional English pudding got its name because it is so easy to make that even a 'fool' can attempt it.

Ingredients

Serves 4

30ml/2 tbsp orange juice
5ml/1 tsp finely shredded orange rind
1kg/2lb (about 10–12 stems) rhubarb,
    chopped
15ml/1 tbsp redcurrant jelly
45ml/3 tbsp caster sugar
150g/5oz ready-to-serve thick and
    creamy custard
150ml/¼ pint/⅔ cup double cream,
    whipped
sweet biscuits, to serve

1 Place the orange juice and rind, the rhubarb, redcurrant jelly and sugar into a saucepan. Cover and simmer gently for about 8 minutes, stirring occasionally, until the rhubarb is just tender but not mushy.

2 Remove the pan from the heat, transfer the rhubarb to a bowl and leave to cool completely. Meanwhile, beat the cream lightly.

3 Drain the cooled rhubarb to remove some of the liquid. Reserve a few pieces of the rhubarb and a little orange rind for decoration. Purée the remaining rhubarb in a food processor or blender, or push through a sieve.

4 Stir the custard into the purée, then fold in the whipped cream. Spoon the fool into individual bowls, cover and chill. Just before serving, top with the reserved fruit and rind. Serve with crisp, sweet biscuits.

Apricot Mousse

This light, fluffy dessert can be made with any dried fruits instead of apricots – try dried peaches, prunes, or apples.

INGREDIENTS

Serves 4

300g/10oz/1½ cups dried apricots
300ml/½ pint/1¼ cups fresh orange juice
200g/7oz/⅞ cup low fat fromage frais
2 egg whites
mint sprigs, to decorate

1 Place the apricots in a saucepan with the orange juice and heat gently until boiling. Cover the pan and simmer gently for 3 minutes.

2 Cool slightly. Place in a food processor or blender and process until smooth. Stir in the fromage frais.

3 Whisk the egg whites until stiff enough to hold soft peaks, then fold into the apricot mixture.

4 Spoon into four stemmed glasses or one large serving dish. Chill before serving, decorated with mint.

―――― COOK'S TIP ――――
For an even quicker version, omit the egg whites and simply swirl together the apricot mixture and fromage frais.

―――― WATCHPOINT ――――
This dessert contains raw egg whites and so shouldn't be served to young children, pregnant women or the sick.

Chocolate Fudge Sundaes

INGREDIENTS

Serves 4

4 scoops each vanilla and coffee
  ice cream
2 small ripe bananas, sliced
whipped cream
toasted flaked almonds

For the sauce

50g/2oz/¼ cup soft light brown sugar
120ml/4fl oz/½ cup golden syrup
45ml/3 tbsp strong black coffee
5ml/1 tsp ground cinnamon
150g/5oz plain chocolate, chopped
85ml/3fl oz/⅓ cup whipping cream
45ml/3 tbsp coffee liqueur (optional)

1 To make the sauce, place the
sugar, syrup, coffee and cinnamon
in a heavy-based saucepan. Bring to
the boil, then boil for about 5 minutes,
stirring constantly.

2 Turn off the heat and stir in the
chocolate. When melted and
smooth, stir in the cream and liqueur,
if using. Leave the sauce to cool
slightly. If made ahead, reheat the
sauce gently until just warm.

3 Fill four glasses with a scoop each
of vanilla and coffee ice cream.

4 Scatter the sliced bananas over the
ice cream. Pour the warm fudge
sauce over the bananas, then top each
sundae with a generous swirl of
whipped cream. Sprinkle with toasted
almonds and serve at once.

VARIATION

Ring the changes by choosing other
flavours of ice cream such as strawberry,
toffee or chocolate. In the summer, substitute raspberries or strawberries for the
bananas, and scatter chopped roasted hazelnuts on top in place of the flaked almonds.

White Chocolate Parfait

INGREDIENTS

Serves 10

225g/8oz white chocolate, chopped
600ml/1 pint/2½ cups whipping
  cream
120ml/4fl oz/½ cup milk
10 egg yolks
15ml/1 tbsp caster sugar
25g/1oz/⅓ cup desiccated coconut
120ml/4fl oz/½ cup canned sweetened
  coconut milk
150g/5oz unsalted macadamia nuts

For the chocolate icing

225g/8oz plain chocolate
75g/3oz/6 tbsp butter
20ml/1 generous tbsp golden syrup
175ml/6fl oz/¾ cup whipping cream
curls of fresh coconut, to decorate

1 Line the base and sides of a 1.4 litre/2⅓ pint/6 cup terrine mould (25 x 10cm/10 x 4in) with clear film.

2 Place the white chocolate and 50ml/2fl oz/¼ cup of the cream in the top of a double boiler or in a heat-proof bowl set over hot water. Stir until melted and smooth. Set aside.

3 Put 250ml/8fl oz/1 cup of the cream and the milk in a pan and bring to boiling point.

4 Meanwhile, whisk the egg yolks and caster sugar together in a large bowl, until thick and pale.

5 Add the hot cream mixture to the yolks, beating constantly. Pour back into the saucepan and cook over a low heat for 2–3 minutes, until thickened. Stir constantly and do not boil. Remove the pan from the heat.

6 Add the melted chocolate, desiccated coconut and coconut milk, then stir well and leave to cool.

7 Whip the remaining cream until thick, then fold into the chocolate and coconut mixture.

8 Put 475ml/16fl oz/2 cups of the parfait mixture in the prepared mould and spread evenly. Cover and freeze for about 2 hours, until just firm. Cover the remaining mixture and chill.

9 Scatter the macadamia nuts evenly over the frozen parfait. Pour in the remaining parfait mixture. Cover the terrine and freeze for 6–8 hours or overnight, until the parfait is firm.

10 To make the icing, melt the chocolate with the butter and syrup in the top of a double boiler set over hot water. Stir occasionally.

11 Heat the cream in a saucepan, until just simmering, then stir into the chocolate mixture. Remove the pan from the heat and leave to cool until lukewarm.

12 To turn out the parfait, wrap the terrine in a hot towel and set it upside-down on a plate. Lift off the terrine mould, then peel off the clear film. Place the parfait on a rack over a baking sheet and pour the chocolate icing evenly over the top. Working quickly, smooth the icing down the sides with a palette knife. Leave to set slightly, then freeze for a further 3–4 hours. Cut into slices using a knife dipped in hot water. Serve, decorated with coconut curls.

Banana and Passion Fruit Whip

This very easy and quickly prepared dessert is delicious served with crisp biscuits.

INGREDIENTS

Serves 4
2 ripe bananas
2 passion fruit
90ml/6 tbsp fromage frais
150ml/¼ pint/⅔ cup double cream
10ml/2 tsp clear honey
shortcake or ginger biscuits, to serve

1 Peel the bananas, then mash them in a bowl to a smooth purée.

2 Halve the passion fruit and scoop out the pulp. Mix with the bananas and fromage frais. Whip the cream with the honey until it forms soft peaks.

3 Carefully fold the cream and honey mixture into the fruit mixture. Spoon into four glass dishes and serve at once with the biscuits.

Coffee Jellies with Amaretti Cream

This impressive dessert is very easy to prepare. For the best results, use a high-roasted Arabica bean, preferably from a specialist coffee shop. Grind the beans until filter-fine, then use to make hot strong coffee.

INGREDIENTS

Serves 4
75g/3oz/6 tbsp caster sugar
450ml/¾ pint/1⅞ cups hot strong coffee
30–45ml/2–3 tbsp dark rum or coffee liqueur
20ml/4 tsp powdered gelatine

For the coffee amaretti cream
150ml/¼ pint/⅔ cup double or whipping cream
15ml/1 tbsp icing sugar, sifted
10–15ml/2–3 tsp instant coffee granules dissolved in 15ml/1 tbsp hot water
6 large amaretti biscuits, crushed

1 Put the sugar in a pan with 75ml/5 tbsp water and stir over a gentle heat until dissolved. Increase the heat and allow the syrup to boil steadily, without stirring, for 3–4 minutes.

2 Stir the hot coffee and rum or coffee liqueur into the syrup. Sprinkle the gelatine over the top and stir until it is completely dissolved.

3 Pour the jelly mixture into four wetted 150ml/¼ pint/⅔ cup moulds, allow to cool and then leave in the fridge for several hours until set.

4 To make the amaretti cream, lightly whip the cream with the icing sugar until it holds stiff peaks. Stir in the coffee, then gently fold in all but 30ml/2 tbsp of the crushed amaretti biscuits.

5 Unmould the jellies on to four individual serving plates and spoon a little of the coffee amaretti cream to one side. Dust over the reserved amaretti crumbs and serve at once.

COOK'S TIP

To ensure that the finished jellies are crystal-clear, filter the coffee grounds through a paper filter.

Chocolate Chestnut Roulade

This moist chocolate sponge has a soft, mousse-like texture as it contains no flour. Don't worry if it cracks as you roll it up – this is typical of a good roulade.

INGREDIENTS

Serves 8

175g/6oz plain chocolate
30ml/2 tbsp strong black coffee
5 eggs, separated
175g/6oz/³⁄₄ cup caster sugar
250ml/8fl oz/1 cup double cream
225g/8oz unsweetened chestnut
  purée
45–60ml/3–4 tbsp icing sugar, plus
  extra for dusting
single cream, to serve

1 Preheat the oven to 180°C/350°F/ Gas 4. Line a 33 x 23cm/13 x 9in Swiss roll tin with non-stick baking paper and brush lightly with oil.

2 Break up the chocolate into a bowl and set over a pan of barely simmering water. Allow the chocolate to melt, then stir until smooth. Remove the bowl from the pan and stir in the coffee. Leave to cool slightly.

3 Whisk the egg yolks and sugar together in a separate bowl, until thick and light, then stir in the cooled chocolate mixture.

4 Whisk the egg whites in another bowl until they hold stiff peaks. Stir a spoonful into the chocolate mixture to lighten it, then gently fold in the rest.

5 Pour the mixture into the prepared tin, and gently spread level. Bake for 20 minutes. Remove the roulade from the oven, then cover the cooked roulade with a clean dish towel and leave to cool in the tin for several hours, or preferably overnight.

6 Whip the cream until it forms soft peaks. Mix together the chestnut purée and icing sugar until smooth, then fold into the whipped cream.

7 Lay a piece of greaseproof paper on the work surface and dust with icing sugar. Turn out the roulade on to the paper and carefully peel off the lining paper. Trim the sides.

8 Gently spread the chestnut cream evenly over the roulade to within 2.5cm/1in of the edges.

9 Using the greaseproof paper to help you, carefully roll up the roulade as tightly and evenly as possible.

10 Chill the roulade for about 2 hours, then sprinkle liberally with icing sugar. Cut into thick slices and serve with a little single cream poured over each slice.

COOK'S TIP

Make sure that you whisk the egg yolks and sugar for at least 5 minutes to incorporate as much air as possible.

PIES AND TARTS

The combination of crisp pastry with a sweet, tangy or creamy filling make pies and tarts a popular pudding choice. Many are delicious hot or cold, and are excellent dished up with custard, a dollop of whipped cream or a scoop or two of ice cream. You'll find plenty of variety to choose from. There are traditional fruit pies filled with apple, walnut and pears, rhubarb, or blueberries; delicious American classics such as Spiced Pumpkin Pie; and new twists on family favourites like Treacle and Oatmeal Tart.

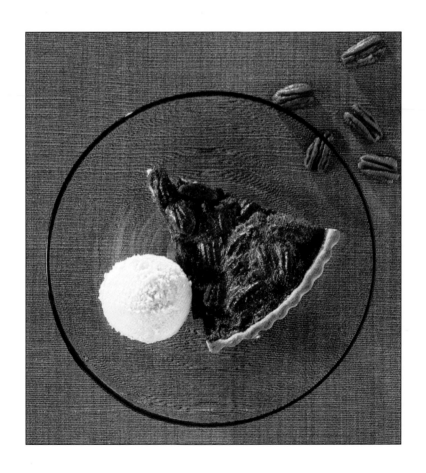

Yorkshire Curd Tart

The distinguishing characteristic of traditional Yorkshire curd tarts is allspice, or 'clove pepper' as it was known locally.

INGREDIENTS

Serves 8
115g/4oz/½ cup butter, diced
225g/8oz/2 cups plain flour
1 egg yolk

For the filling
large pinch of ground allspice
90g/3½oz/½ cup soft light brown
   sugar
3 eggs, beaten
grated rind and juice of 1 lemon
40g/1½oz/3 tbsp butter, melted
450g/1lb curd cheese
75g/3oz/scant ½ cup raisins or
   sultanas

1 Toss the butter in the flour, then rub it in until the mixture resembles breadcrumbs. Stir the egg yolk into the flour mixture with a little water to bind the dough together.

2 Turn the dough on to a lightly floured surface, knead lightly and briefly, then form into a ball. Roll out the pastry thinly and use to line a 20cm/8in fluted loose-bottomed flan tin. Chill for 15 minutes.

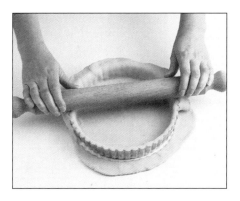

3 Preheat the oven to 190°C/375°F/ Gas 5. To make the filling, mix the ground allspice with the sugar, then stir in the eggs, lemon rind and juice, melted butter, curd cheese and raisins or sultanas.

4 Pour the filling into the pastry case, then bake for about 40 minutes until the pastry is cooked and the filling is lightly set and golden brown. Serve still slightly warm, cut into wedges, with cream, if you like.

Bakewell Tart

Although the pastry base makes this a tart, the original recipe calls it a pudding.

INGREDIENTS

Serves 4
225g/8oz ready-made puff pastry
30ml/2 tbsp raspberry or apricot jam
2 eggs
2 egg yolks
115g/4oz/generous ½ cup caster sugar
115g/4oz/½ cup butter, melted
50g/2oz/⅔ cup ground almonds
few drops of almond essence
icing sugar, for sifting

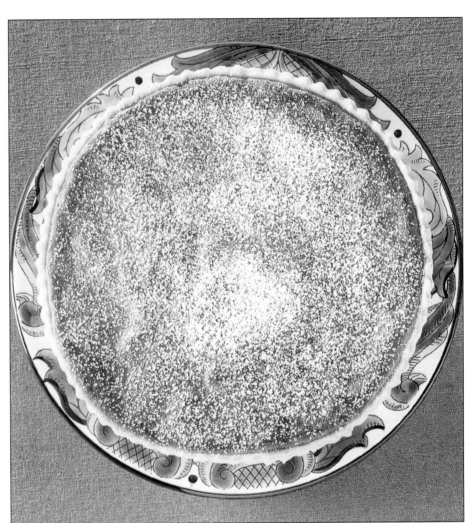

1 Preheat the oven to 200°C/400°F/ Gas 6. Roll out the pastry on a lightly floured surface and use it to line an 18cm/7in pie plate or loose-based flan tin. Spread the jam over the bottom of the pastry case.

2 Whisk the eggs, egg yolks and sugar together in a large bowl until thick and pale.

3 Gently stir the butter, ground almonds and almond essence into the mixture.

4 Pour the mixture into the pastry case and bake for 30 minutes, until the filling is just set and browned. Sift icing sugar over the top before eating hot, warm or cold.

COOK'S TIP

Since this pastry case isn't baked blind first, place a baking sheet in the oven while it preheats, then place the flan tin on the hot sheet. This will ensure that the bottom of the pastry case cooks right through.

VARIATION

Ground hazelnuts are increasingly available and make an interesting change to the almonds in this tart. If you are going to grind shelled hazelnuts yourself, first roast them in the oven for 10–15 minutes to bring out their flavour.

Rhubarb Pie

INGREDIENTS

Serves 6

175g/6oz/1½ cups plain flour
2.5ml/½ tsp salt
10ml/2 tsp caster sugar
75g/3oz/6 tbsp cold butter or margarine
50ml/2fl oz/¼ cup or more iced water
30ml/2 tbsp single cream

For the filling

1kg/2lb fresh rhubarb, cut into
    2.5cm/1in slices
30ml/2 tbsp cornflour
1 egg
275g/10oz/1½ cups caster sugar
15ml/1 tbsp grated orange rind

1 To make the pastry, sift the flour, salt and sugar into a bowl. Using a pastry blender or two knives, cut the butter or margarine into the dry ingredients as quickly as possible until the mixture resembles breadcrumbs.

2 Sprinkle the flour mixture with the iced water and mix until the dough just holds together. If the dough is too crumbly, add a little more water, 15ml/1 tbsp at a time.

—————— COOK'S TIP ——————
Use milk in place of the single cream to glaze the pie, if you prefer. Or for a crisp crust, brush the pastry with water and sprinkle with caster sugar instead.

3 Gather the dough into a ball, flatten into a round, place in a polythene bag and chill for 20 minutes.

4 Roll out the pastry between two sheets of greaseproof paper to a 3mm/⅛in thickness. Use to line a 23cm/9in pie dish or tin. Trim all around, leaving a 1cm/½in overhang. Fold the overhang under the edge and flute. Chill the pastry case and trimmings for at least 30 minutes.

5 To make the filling, put the rhubarb in a bowl, sprinkle with the cornflour and toss to coat.

6 Preheat the oven to 220°C/425°F/ Gas 7. Beat the egg with the sugar in a bowl until thoroughly blended, then mix in the orange rind.

7 Stir the sugar mixture into the rhubarb and mix well, then spoon the fruit into the pastry case.

8 Roll out the pastry trimmings. Stamp out decorative shapes with a biscuit cutter or cut shapes with a small knife, using a cardboard template as a guide, if your prefer.

9 Arrange the pastry shapes on top of the pie. Brush the shapes and the edge of the pastry case with cream.

10 Bake the pie for 30 minutes. Reduce the oven temperature to 160°C/325°F/Gas 3 and continue baking for a further 15–20 minutes, until the pastry is golden brown and the rhubarb is tender. Serve the pie hot with cream.

American Spiced Pumpkin Pie

INGREDIENTS

Serves 4–6

175g/6oz/1½ cups plain flour
pinch of salt
75g/3oz/6 tbsp unsalted butter
15ml/1 tbsp caster sugar
450g/1lb/4 cups peeled fresh pumpkin, cubed, or 400g/14oz/2 cups
  canned pumpkin, drained
115g/4oz/⅝ cup soft light brown sugar
1.25ml/¼ tsp salt
1.25ml/¼ tsp ground allspice
2.5ml/½ tsp ground cinnamon
2.5ml/½ tsp ground ginger
2 eggs, lightly beaten
120ml/4fl oz/½ cup double cream
whipped cream, to serve

1 Place the flour in a bowl with the salt and butter and rub in with your fingertips until the mixture resembles breadcrumbs (or use a food processor).

2 Stir in the sugar and add about 30–45ml/2–3 tbsp water and mix to a soft dough. Knead the dough lightly on a floured surface. Flatten out into a round, wrap in a polythene bag and chill for about 1 hour.

3 Preheat the oven to 200°C/400°F/ Gas 6 with a baking sheet inside. If you are using raw pumpkin for the pie, steam for 15 minutes until quite tender, then leave to cool completely. Purée the steamed or canned pumpkin in a food processor or blender until very smooth.

4 Roll out the pastry quite thinly and use to line a 23.5cm/9½in (measured across the top) x 2.5cm/1in deep pie tin. Trim off any excess pastry and reserve for the decoration. Prick the base of the pastry case with a fork.

5 Cut as many leaf shapes as you can from the excess pastry and make vein markings with the back of a knife on each. Brush the edge of the pastry with water and stick the leaves all round the edge. Chill.

6 In a bowl mix together the pumpkin purée, sugar, salt, spices, eggs and cream and pour into the pastry case.

7 Place on the preheated baking sheet and bake for 15 minutes. Then reduce the temperature to 180°C/ 350°F/ Gas 4 and cook for a further 30 minutes, or until the filling is set and the pastry golden. Serve the pie warm with whipped cream.

Almond Syrup Tart

INGREDIENTS

Serves 6

75g/3oz fresh white breadcrumbs
225g/8oz golden syrup
finely grated rind of ½ lemon
10ml/2 tsp lemon juice
23cm/9in shortcrust pastry case
25g/1oz flaked almonds

1 Preheat the oven to 200°C/400°F/
Gas 6. In a mixing bowl, combine
the breadcrumbs with the golden syrup
and the lemon rind and juice.

2 Spoon into the pastry case and
spread out evenly.

3 Sprinkle the flaked almonds evenly
over the top.

4 Brush the pastry with milk to
glaze, if you like. Bake for 25–30
minutes or until the pastry and filling
are golden brown.

5 Remove to a wire rack to cool.
Serve warm or cold, with cream,
custard or ice cream.

COOK'S TIP

For Walnut Syrup Tart, replace the
almonds with chopped walnuts. For
Ginger Syrup Tart, mix 5ml/1 tsp ground
ginger with the breadcrumbs before
adding the syrup and lemon rind and
juice. Omit the nuts if liked. For Coconut
Syrup Tart, replace 25g/1oz of the breadcrumbs with 40g/1½oz of desiccated
coconut.

Peanut Butter Tart

INGREDIENTS

Serves 8

175g/6oz digestive biscuits, crushed
50g/2oz/¼ cup soft light brown sugar
75g/3oz/6 tbsp butter or margarine,
  melted
whipped cream or ice cream, to serve

For the filling

3 egg yolks
90g/3½oz/½ cup caster sugar
50g/2oz/¼ cup soft light brown sugar
25g/1oz/¼ cup cornflour
600ml/1 pint/2½ cups canned
  evaporated milk
25g/1oz/2 tbsp unsalted butter or
  margarine
7.5ml/1½ tsp vanilla essence
115g/4oz crunchy peanut butter
75g/3oz/¾ cup icing sugar

1 Preheat the oven to 180°C/350°F/
Gas 4. Grease a 23cm/9in pie dish.

2 Mix together the biscuit crumbs,
sugar and butter or margarine in a
bowl and blend well. Spread the mixture in the prepared dish, pressing the
mixture evenly over the base and sides
with your fingertips.

3 Bake the crumb crust for 10 minutes. Remove from the oven and
leave to cool. Leave the oven on.

4 To make the filling, mix together
the egg yolks, caster and brown
sugars and cornflour in a heavy-based
saucepan using a wooden spoon,

5 Slowly whisk in the milk, then
cook over a medium heat for about
8–10 minutes, stirring constantly, until
the mixture thickens. Reduce the heat
to very low and cook for a further 3–4
minutes, until the mixture is very thick.

6 Beat in the butter or margarine
and the vanilla essence. Remove
the pan from the heat, then cover the
surface loosely with clear film and cool.

----- COOK'S TIP -----
If preferred, use an equal amount of finely
crushed ginger snaps in place of digestive
biscuits for the crumb crust. Or make the
pie with a ready-made pastry case.

7 Combine the peanut butter with
the icing sugar in a small bowl,
working with your fingertips to blend
the ingredients to the consistency of
fine breadcrumbs.

8 Sprinkle all but 45ml/3 tbsp of the
peanut butter crumbs evenly over
the base of the crumb crust.

9 Pour in the filling, spreading it
into an even layer, then sprinkle
with the remaining crumbs and bake
for 15 minutes. Leave the pie to cool
for at least 1 hour. Serve with whipped
cream or ice cream.

Mississippi Pecan Pie

INGREDIENTS

Makes a 20cm/8in pie

For the pastry
115g/4oz/1 cup plain flour
50g/2oz/4 tbsp butter, cubed
25g/1oz/2 tbsp caster sugar
1 egg yolk

For the filling
175g/6oz/5 tbsp golden syrup
50g/2oz/⅓ cup dark muscovado
  sugar
50g/2oz/4 tbsp butter
3 eggs, lightly beaten
2.5ml/½ tsp vanilla essence
150g/5oz/1¼ cups pecan nuts
fresh cream or ice cream, to serve

1 Place the flour in a bowl and add the butter. Rub in the butter with your fingertips until the mixture resembles breadcrumbs, then stir in the sugar, egg yolk and about 30ml/2 tbsp cold water. Mix to a dough and knead lightly on a floured surface until smooth.

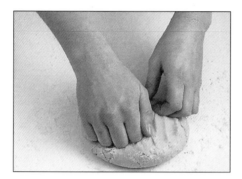

2 Roll out the pastry and use to line a 20cm/8in loose-based fluted flan tin. Prick the base, then line with greaseproof paper and fill with baking beans. Chill for 30 minutes. Preheat the oven to 200°C/400°F/Gas 6.

3 Bake the pastry case for 10 minutes. Remove the paper and beans and bake for 5 minutes. Reduce the oven temperature to 180°C/350°F/Gas 4.

4 Meanwhile, heat the syrup, sugar and butter in a pan until the sugar dissolves. Remove from the heat and cool slightly. Whisk in the eggs and vanilla essence and stir in the pecans.

5 Pour into the pastry case and bake for 35–40 minutes, until the filling is set. Serve with cream or ice cream.

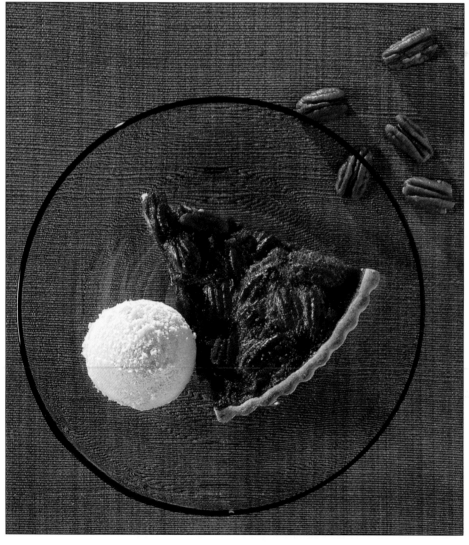

Walnut and Pear Lattice Pie

INGREDIENTS

Serves 6–8

350g/12oz shortcrust pastry
1kg/2lb pears, peeled, cored and thinly
    sliced
50g/2oz caster sugar
25g/1oz plain flour
2.5ml/½ tsp grated lemon rind
25g/1oz raisins or sultanas
25g/1oz walnuts, chopped
2.5ml/½ tsp ground cinnamon
50g/2oz icing sugar
15ml/1 tbsp lemon juice
about 10ml/2 tsp cold water

1 Preheat the oven to 190°C/375°F/
Gas 5. Roll out half of the pastry
and use to line a 23cm/9in tin that is
about 5cm/2in deep.

2 Combine the pears, caster sugar,
flour and lemon rind in a bowl.
Toss gently until the fruit is evenly
coated with the dry ingredients. Mix
in the raisins, nuts and cinnamon.

_____ COOK'S TIP _____

For a simple cutout lattice top, roll out the
dough for the top into a circle. Using a
small pastry cutter, cut out shapes in a pattern, spacing them evenly and not too
close together.

3 Put the pear filling into the pastry
case and spread it evenly.

4 Roll out the remaining pastry on a
floured surface and use to make a
lattice top.

5 Bake the pie for 55 minutes or
until the pastry is golden brown.

6 Combine the icing sugar, lemon
juice and water in a bowl and stir
until smoothly blended.

7 Remove the pie from the oven.
Drizzle the icing sugar glaze evenly
over the top of the pie, on pastry and
filling. Leave the pie to cool, set on a
wire rack, before serving.

Grilled Oranges with Spiced Cream

INGREDIENTS

Serves 4

3 large oranges
15–30ml/1–2 tbsp demerara sugar
150ml/¼ pint/⅔ cup thick or soured
  cream, crème fraîche or
  Greek-style yogurt
5ml/1 tsp mixed spice
few drops vanilla essence
caster sugar, to taste

1 Cut away all the orange rind and
white pith using a sharp knife, saving any of the juices. Cut the oranges
into thick slices and arrange these on
foil in a grill pan.

2 Sprinkle the orange slices with
demerara sugar. Whisk the cream,
crème fraîche or yogurt until smooth,
then blend in the mixed spice and vanilla essence and any orange juice. Chill.

3 Place the orange slices under a very
hot grill and grill until browned and
bubbling. Transfer the orange slices to
serving plates and serve at once with
the chilled spiced cream.

Treacle and Oatmeal Tart

Treacle tart always evokes childhood memories. This one, however, has some concessions to
these health-conscious days with
added crunch and fibre. It's just
as good, though.

INGREDIENTS

Serves 6–8

115g/4oz/1 cup plain flour
50g/2oz/⅔ cup rolled oats
pinch of salt
115g/4oz/½ cup butter or margarine
150g/5oz/6 tbsp golden syrup
25g/1oz/2 tbsp black treacle
grated rind and juice of 1 orange
75g/3oz/1½ cups soft white bread or
  cake crumbs

1 Place the flour, rolled oats, salt
and butter or margarine in a food
processor and process on high for
½–1 minute, until well blended.

2 Turn into a bowl and stir in sufficient water (60–75ml/4–5 tbsp) to
bring the pastry together. Knead lightly
until smooth, wrap in clear film and
chill for 10–20 minutes.

3 Place the syrup, treacle, orange rind
and juice in a small pan and warm
through gently. Then stir in the crumbs.
Preheat the oven to 190°C/375°F/Gas 5.

4 Roll out the pastry on a floured
surface to a 23cm/9in round and
use to line a shallow 20cm/8in pie
plate. Trim the edges neatly, then re-roll
the trimmings, cut out leaves and use to
decorate the edges.

5 Spread the filling in the pastry case
and bake for 25–30 minutes, or
until the pastry is crisp.

Pear and Blueberry Pie

INGREDIENTS

Serves 4

225g/8oz/2 cups plain flour
pinch of salt
50g/2oz/4 tbsp lard, cubed
50g/2oz/4 tbsp butter, cubed
675g/1½lb blueberries
30ml/2 tbsp caster sugar
15ml/1 tbsp arrowroot
2 ripe, but firm pears, peeled, cored
   and sliced
2.5ml/½ tsp ground cinnamon
grated rind of ½ lemon
beaten egg white, to glaze
caster sugar, for sprinkling
crème fraîche, to serve

1 Sift the flour and salt into a bowl and rub in the lard and butter until the mixture resembles fine breadcrumbs. Stir in 45ml/3 tbsp cold water and mix to a dough. Chill for 30 minutes.

2 Place 225g/8oz of the blueberries in a pan with the sugar. Cover and cook gently until the blueberries have softened. Press through a nylon sieve.

3 Blend the arrowroot with 30ml/2 tbsp cold water and add to the blueberry purée. Bring to the boil, stirring until thickened. Cool slightly.

4 Place a baking sheet in the oven and preheat to 190°C/375°F/Gas 5. Roll out just over half the pastry on a lightly floured surface and use to line a 20cm/8in shallow pie dish or plate.

5 Mix together the remaining blueberries, the pears, cinnamon and lemon rind and spoon into the dish. Pour over the blueberry purée.

6 Roll out the remaining pastry and use to cover the pie. Make a small slit in the centre. Brush with egg white and sprinkle with caster sugar. Bake the pie on the hot baking sheet, for 40–45 minutes, until golden. Serve warm with crème fraîche.

Blueberry Pie

INGREDIENTS

Serves 6–8

350g/12oz shortcrust pastry
500g/1¼lb blueberries
165g/5½oz caster sugar
45ml/3 tbsp plain flour
5ml/1 tsp grated orange rind
pinch of grated nutmeg
30ml/2 tbsp orange juice
5ml/1 tsp lemon juice

1 Preheat the oven to 190°C/375°F/ Gas 5. Roll out half of the pastry and use to line a 23cm/9in pie tin that is about 5cm/2in deep.

2 Combine the blueberries, 150g/ 5oz of the sugar, the flour, orange rind and nutmeg in a bowl. Toss the mixture gently to coat the fruit evenly with the dry ingredients.

3 Pour the blueberry mixture into the pastry case and spread it evenly. Sprinkle over the citrus juices.

4 Roll out the remaining pastry and cover the pie. Cut out small decorative shapes or cut two or three slits for steam vents. Finish the edge.

5 Brush the top lightly with water and sprinkle evenly with the remaining caster sugar.

6 Bake for about 45 minutes or until the pastry is golden brown. Serve warm or at room temperature.

Apple Pie

INGREDIENTS

Serves 8

900g/2lb tart apples, such as Granny
   Smith, peeled, cored and sliced
15ml/1 tbsp fresh lemon juice
5ml/1 tsp vanilla essence
115g/4oz caster sugar
2.5ml/½ tsp ground cinnamon
40g/1½oz butter or margarine
1 egg yolk
10ml/2 tsp whipping cream

For the crust

225g/8oz/2 cups plain flour
pinch of salt
175g/6oz white cooking fat
60–75ml/4–5 tbsp iced water
15ml/1 tbsp quick-cooking tapioca

1 Preheat the oven to 230°C/450°F/
Gas 8. To make the pastry, sift the
flour and salt into a mixing bowl. Rub
in the cooking fat until the mixture
resembles coarse crumbs.

2 Sprinkle in the water, 15ml/1 tbsp
at a time, tossing lightly with your
fingertips or with a fork until the
dough will form a ball.

3 Divide the dough in half and shape
each half into a ball. On a lightly
floured surface, roll out one of the balls
to a 30cm/12in round.

4 Use it to line a 23cm/9in pie tin,
easing the dough in and being
careful not to stretch it. Trim off the
excess dough and use the trimmings for
decorating. Sprinkle the tapioca over
the base of the pastry case.

5 Roll out the remaining dough to a
3mm/⅛in thickness. With a sharp
knife, cut out eight large leaf-shapes. Cut
the trimmings into small leaf shapes.
Score the leaves with the back of the
knife to mark veins.

6 In a bowl, toss the apples with the
lemon juice, vanilla essence, sugar
and cinnamon. Fill the pastry case with
the apple mixture and dot with the
butter or margarine.

7 Arrange the large pastry leaves in a
decorative pattern on top, then
decorate the edge with small leaves.

8 Mix together the egg yolk and
cream and brush over the leaves.
Bake for 10 minutes, then reduce the
heat to 180°C/350°F/Gas 4, and continue baking for 35–45 minutes until the
pastry is golden brown. Remove the pie
from the oven and leave to cool in the
tin, set on a wire rack.

Mississippi Mud Pie

INGREDIENTS

Serves 8

75g/3oz plain chocolate
50g/2oz/4 tbsp butter or margarine
15ml/3 tbsp golden syrup
3 eggs, beaten
150g/5oz/⅔ cup caster sugar
5ml/1 tsp vanilla essence
115g/4oz milk chocolate
475ml/16fl oz/2 cups whipping cream

For the crust

165g/5½oz/1⅓ cups plain flour
pinch of salt
115g/4oz white cooking fat
30–45ml/2–3 tbsp iced water

1 Preheat the oven to 220°C/425°F/ Gas 7. To make the crust, sift the flour and salt into a mixing bowl. Rub in the fat until the mixture resembles coarse crumbs. Sprinkle in the water, 15ml/1 tbsp at a time. Toss lightly with your fingers or a fork until the dough will form a ball.

2 On a lightly floured surface, roll out the dough. Use to line a 20–23cm/8–9in pie tin, easing in the dough and being careful not to stretch it. With your thumb and fingertips, make a fluted edge.

3 Using a fork, prick the base and sides of the pie case all over. Bake for 10–15 minutes until lightly browned. Leave to cool, in the tin, on a wire rack.

4 In a heatproof bowl set over a pan of simmering water, melt the plain chocolate, butter or margarine and golden syrup. Remove the bowl from the heat and stir in the eggs, sugar and vanilla essence.

5 Reduce the oven temperature to 180°C/350°F/Gas 4. Pour the chocolate mixture into the baked crust. Bake for 35–40 minutes until the filling is set. Leave to cool completely.

6 To make the decoration, use the heat of your hands to soften the milk chocolate slightly. Draw the blade of a swivel-headed vegetable peeler along the side of the chocolate bar to shave off short, wide curls. Chill the chocolate curls until needed.

7 Before serving, lightly whip the cream until soft peaks form. Using a rubber spatula, spread the cream over the surface of the chocolate filling. Decorate with the chocolate curls.

Banana Cream Pie

INGREDIENTS

Serves 6

200g/7oz ginger biscuits, finely
   crushed
65g/2½oz/5 tbsp butter, melted
2.5ml/½ tsp grated nutmeg or ground
   cinnamon
175g/6oz ripe bananas, mashed
350g/12oz cream cheese, at room
   temperature
60ml/4 tbsp thick yogurt or soured cream
45ml/3 tbsp dark rum or 5ml/1 tsp
   vanilla essence

For the topping

250ml/8fl oz/1 cup whipping cream
3–4 bananas

1 Preheat the oven to 190°C/375°F/
Gas 5. In a bowl, mix together the
biscuit crumbs, butter and spice with a
wooden spoon.

2 Press the crumb mixture into a
23cm/9in pie tin, building up
thick sides with a neat edge. Bake for
5 minutes. Leave to cool, in the pan,
on a wire rack.

3 With an electric mixer, beat the
mashed bananas with the cream
cheese. Fold in the yogurt or soured
cream and rum or vanilla essence.
Spread the filling in the crumb crust.
Chill at least 4 hours or overnight.

4 For the topping, whip the cream
until soft peaks form. Spread on
the pie filling. Slice the bananas and
arrange on top in a decorative pattern.

FRUIT DESSERTS

Light, tangy and refreshing, simple fruit desserts are particularly appealing after a rich or filling main course. You'll find some enticing treats here, such as Hot Spiced Bananas, Baked Peaches with Raspberry Sauce, and Tropical Fruits in Cinnamon Syrup, as well as old favourites such as baked apples, poached pears, and a selection of hot fruit compôtes to try. And, if the meal is a little lighter, Blueberry Pancakes, Fruity Ricotta Creams, or a rich Raspberry Trifle will go down well with everyone.

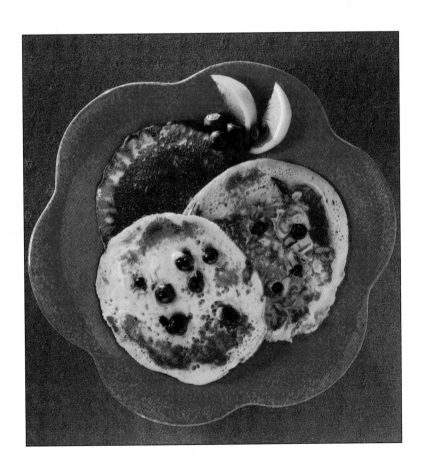

Baked Apples with Apricots

INGREDIENTS

Serves 6

75g/3oz/½ cup chopped, ready-to-eat
   dried apricots
50g/2oz/½ cup chopped walnuts
5ml/1 tsp grated lemon rind
2.5ml/¼ tsp ground cinnamon
80g/3½oz/½ cup soft light brown sugar
15g/1oz/2 tbsp butter, at room temperature
6 large eating apples
15ml/1 tbsp melted butter

1 Place the apricots, walnuts, lemon rind and cinnamon in a bowl. Add the sugar and butter and stir until thoroughly mixed.

2 Preheat the oven to 190°C/375°F/ Gas 5. Core the apples, without cutting all the way through to the base. Peel the top of each apple and slightly widen the top of each opening to make room for the filling.

3 Spoon the filling into the apples, packing it down lightly.

4 Place the stuffed apples in an oven-proof dish large enough to hold them comfortably side by side.

5 Brush the apples with the melted butter. Bake for 40–45 minutes, until they are tender. Serve hot.

Spiced Pears in Cider

Any variety of pear can be used for cooking, but it is best to choose firm pears for this recipe, or they will break up easily – Conference are a good choice.

INGREDIENTS 🍎

Serves 4

4 medium firm pears
250ml/8fl oz/1 cup dry cider
thinly pared strip of lemon rind
1 cinnamon stick
30ml/2 tbsp brown sugar
5ml/1 tsp arrowroot
ground cinnamon, to sprinkle
low-fat fromage frais, to serve

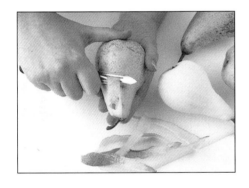

1 Peel the pears thinly, leaving them whole with the stems on. Place in a pan with the cider, lemon rind, and cinnamon. Cover and simmer gently, turning the pears occasionally for 15–20 minutes, or until tender.

2 Lift out the pears. Boil the syrup, uncovered, to reduce by about half. Remove the lemon rind and cinnamon stick, then stir in the sugar.

3 Mix the arrowroot with 15ml/ 1 tbsp cold water in a small bowl until smooth, then stir into the syrup. Bring to the boil and stir over the heat until thickened and clear.

4 Pour the sauce over the pears and sprinkle with ground cinnamon. Leave to cool slightly, then serve warm with low-fat fromage frais.

COOK'S TIP

Whole pears look very impressive, but if you prefer, they can be halved and cored before cooking. This will reduce the cooking time slightly.

VARIATIONS

Other fruits can be poached in this spicy liquid; try apples, peaches or nectarines. Cook the fruit whole or cut in half or quarters. The apples are best peeled before poaching, but you can cook the peaches and nectarines with their skins on.

Greek Fig and Honey Pudding

A quick and easy pudding made from fresh or canned figs topped with thick and creamy Greek yogurt, drizzled with honey and sprinkled with pistachio nuts.

INGREDIENTS

Serves 4

4 fresh or canned figs
2 x 225g/8oz tubs/2 cups Greek strained yogurt
60ml/4 tbsp clear honey
30ml/2 tbsp chopped pistachio nuts

1 Chop the figs and place in the bottom of four stemmed glasses or deep, individual dessert bowls.

2 Top each glass or bowl of figs with half a tub (½ cup) of the Greek yogurt. Chill until ready to serve.

3 Just before serving drizzle 15ml/1 tbsp of honey over each one and sprinkle with the pistachio nuts.

COOK'S TIP

Look out for specialist honeys made from the nectar of flowers like lavender, clover, acacia, heather, rosemary and thyme.

Russian Fruit Compôte

This fruit pudding is traditionally called *Kissel* and is made from the thickened juice of stewed red or blackcurrants. This recipe uses the whole fruit with added blackberry liqueur.

INGREDIENTS

Serves 4

225g/8oz/2 cups red or blackcurrants or a mixture of both
225g/8oz/2 cups raspberries
150ml/¼ pint/⅔ cup water
50g/2oz/4 tbsp caster sugar
22.5ml/1½ tbsp arrowroot
15–30ml/1–2 tbsp Crème de Mûre
Greek yogurt, to serve

1 Place the red or blackcurrants and raspberries, water and sugar in a pan. Cover the pan and cook gently over a low heat for 12–15 minutes, until the fruit is soft.

2 Blend the arrowroot with a little water in a small bowl and stir into the hot fruit mixture. Bring the fruit mixture back to the boil, stirring all the time until thickened and smooth.

3 Remove the pan from the heat and leave the fruit compôte to cool slightly, then gently stir in the Crème de Mûre.

4 Pour the compôte into four glass serving bowls and leave until cold, then chill until required. Serve topped with spoonfuls of Greek yogurt.

COOK'S TIP

Crème de Mûre is a blackberry liqueur available from large supermarkets – you could use Crème de Cassis instead.

Blueberry Pancakes

These are rather like the thick American breakfast pancakes – though they can, of course, be eaten at any time of the day.

INGREDIENTS

Makes 6–8
115g/4oz/1 cup self-raising flour
pinch of salt
45–60ml/3–4 tbsp caster sugar
2 eggs
120ml/4fl oz/½ cup milk
15–30ml/1–2 tbsp oil
115g/4oz fresh or frozen blueberries
maple syrup, to serve

1 Sift the flour into a bowl with the salt and sugar. Beat together the eggs thoroughly. Make a well in the middle of the flour and stir in the eggs.

2 Gradually blend in a little of the milk to make a smooth batter. Then whisk in the rest of the milk and whisk for 1–2 minutes. Allow to rest for 20–30 minutes.

3 Heat a few drops of oil in a pancake pan or heavy-based frying pan until just hazy. Pour on about 30ml/2 tbsp of the batter and swirl the batter around until it makes an even shape.

4 Cook for 2–3 minutes and when almost set on top, sprinkle over 15–30ml/1–2 tbsp blueberries. As soon as the base is loose and golden brown, turn the pancake over.

5 Cook on the second side for only about 1 minute, until golden and crisp. Slide the pancake on to a plate and serve drizzled with maple syrup. Continue with the rest of the batter.

COOK'S TIP

Instead of blueberries you could use fresh or frozen blackberries or raspberries. If you use canned fruit, make sure it is very well drained or the liquid will run and colour the pancakes.

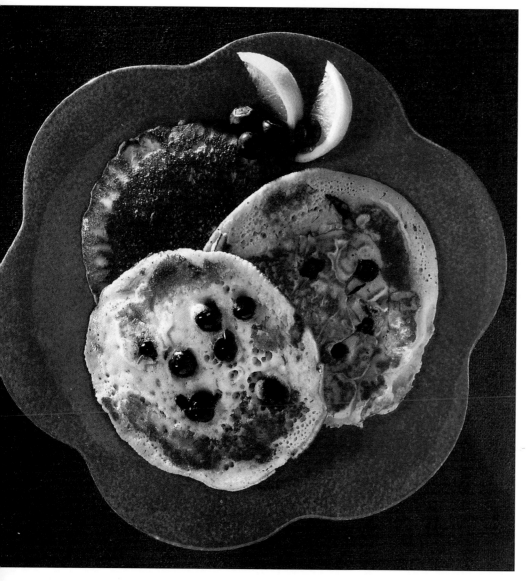

Apple Soufflé Omelette

Apples sautéed until they are slightly caramelized make a delicious autumn filling – you could use fresh raspberries or strawberries in the summer.

INGREDIENTS

Serves 2
4 eggs, separated
30ml/2 tbsp single cream
15ml/1 tbsp caster sugar
15g/½oz/1 tbsp butter
icing sugar, for dredging

For the filling
1 eating apple, peeled, cored and sliced
25g/1oz/2 tbsp butter
30ml/2 tbsp soft light brown sugar
45ml/3 tbsp single cream

1 To make the filling, sauté the apple slices in the butter and sugar until just tender. Stir in the cream and keep warm, while making the omelette.

2 Place the egg yolks in a bowl with the cream and sugar and beat well. Whisk the egg whites until stiff, then fold into the yolk mixture.

3 Melt the butter in a large heavy-based frying pan, pour in the soufflé mixture and spread evenly. Cook for 1 minute until golden underneath, then place under a hot grill to brown the top.

4 Slide the omelette on to a plate, add the apple mixture, then fold over. Sift the icing sugar over thickly, then mark in a criss-cross pattern with a hot metal skewer. Serve immediately.

Ruby Plum Mousse

INGREDIENTS

Serves 6

450g/1lb ripe red plums
45ml/3 tbsp granulated sugar
60ml/4 tbsp ruby port
15ml/1 tbsp/1 sachet powdered
  gelatine
3 eggs, separated
115g/4oz/½ cup caster sugar
150ml/¼ pint/⅔ cup double cream
skinned and chopped pistachio nuts,
  to decorate
cinnamon biscuits, to serve (optional)

1 Place the plums and granulated sugar in a pan with 30ml/2 tbsp water. Cook over a low heat until softened. Press the fruit through a sieve to remove the stones and skins. Leave to cool, then stir in the port.

2 Put 45ml/3 tbsp water in a small bowl, sprinkle over the gelatine and leave to soften. Stand the bowl in a pan of hot water and leave until dissolved. Stir into the plum purée.

3 Place the egg yolks and caster sugar in a bowl and whisk until thick and mousse-like. Fold in the plum purée, then whip the cream and fold in gently.

4 Whisk the egg whites until they hold stiff peaks, then carefully fold in using a metal spoon. Divide among six glasses and chill until set.

5 Decorate the mousses with chopped pistachio nuts and serve with crisp cinnamon biscuits, if liked.

—————— COOK'S TIP ——————
To make a non-alcoholic version, use red grape juice in place of the port.

Warm Autumn Compôte

A simple yet quite sophisticated dessert using autumnal fruits.

INGREDIENTS

Serves 4

75g/3oz/6 tbsp caster sugar
1 bottle red wine
1 vanilla pod, split
1 strip pared lemon rind
4 pears
2 purple figs, quartered
225g/8oz raspberries
lemon juice, to taste

1 Put the sugar and wine in a large pan and heat gently until the sugar is dissolved. Add the vanilla pod and lemon rind and bring to the boil, then simmer for 5 minutes.

2 Peel and halve the pears, then scoop out the cores, using a melon baller. Add the pears to the syrup and poach for 15 minutes, turning the pears several times so they colour evenly.

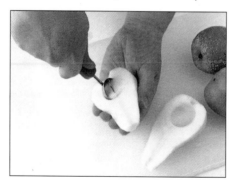

3 Add the figs and poach for a further 5 minutes, until the fruits are tender.

4 Transfer the poached pears and figs to a serving bowl using a slotted spoon, then scatter over the raspberries.

5 Return the syrup to the heat and boil rapidly to reduce slightly and concentrate the flavour. Add a little lemon juice to taste. Strain the syrup over the fruits and serve warm.

Hot Spiced Bananas

INGREDIENTS

Serves 6

6 ripe bananas
200g/7oz/1 cup light brown sugar,
  firmly packed
250ml/8fl oz/1 cup unsweetened
  pineapple juice
125ml/4fl oz/½ cup dark rum
2 cinnamon sticks
12 whole cloves

1 Preheat the oven to 180°C/350°F/
Gas 4. Grease a 23cm/9in shallow
baking dish.

2 Peel the bananas and cut them into
2.5cm/1in pieces on the diagonal.
Arrange the banana pieces evenly over
the base of the prepared baking dish.

3 In a saucepan, combine the sugar
and pineapple juice. Cook over
medium heat until the sugar has dissolved, stirring occasionally.

4 Add the rum, cinnamon sticks, and
cloves. Bring to the boil, then
remove the pan from the heat.

5 Pour the spicy pineapple mixture
over the bananas. Bake for 25–30
minutes until the bananas are very tender and hot. Serve hot.

Baked Peaches with Raspberry Sauce

INGREDIENTS

Serves 6

40g/1½oz/3 tbsp unsalted butter, at
   room temperature
40g/1½oz/¼ cup caster sugar
1 egg, beaten
40g/1½oz/½ cup ground almonds
6 ripe peaches

For the sauce

150g/5oz raspberries
15g/½oz/1 tbsp icing sugar
15ml/1 tbsp raspberry liqueur
raspberries and bay leaves, to decorate

1 Beat the butter with the sugar until
light and fluffy, then beat in the
egg. Add the ground almonds and beat
just enough to blend together well.

2 Preheat the oven to 180°C/350°F/
Gas 4. Halve the peaches and
remove the stones. With a spoon, scrape
out a little of the flesh from each peach
half, slightly enlarging the hollow left by
the stone. Reserve the excess peach
flesh for the sauce.

3 Place the peach halves on a baking
sheet (if necessary, secure with
crumpled foil to keep them steady) and
fill the hollow in each peach half with
the almond mixture.

4 Bake for about 30 minutes, until
the almond filling is puffed and
golden and the peaches are very tender.

5 Meanwhile, to make the sauce,
place the raspberries, icing sugar
and liqueur in a food processor or
blender. Add the reserved peach flesh
and process until smooth. Press through
a sieve to remove the seeds.

6 Leave the peaches to cool slightly,
then serve with the raspberry sauce.
Decorate each serving with a few
raspberries and bay leaves.

Cherries Jubilee

Fresh cherries are wonderful cooked lightly to serve hot over ice cream. Children especially will love this dessert.

INGREDIENTS

Serves 4

450g/1lb red or black cherries
115g/4oz/½ cup granulated sugar
pared rind of 1 lemon
15ml/1 tbsp arrowroot
60ml/4 tbsp Kirsch
vanilla ice cream, to serve

COOK'S TIP

If you don't have a cherry stoner, simply push the stones through with a skewer. Remember to save the juice to use in the recipe.

1 Stone the cherries over a pan to catch the juice. Drop the stones into the pan as you work.

2 Add the sugar, lemon rind and 300ml/½ pint/1¼ cups water to the pan. Stir over a low heat until the sugar dissolves, then bring to the boil and simmer for 10 minutes. Strain the syrup, then return to the pan. Add the cherries and cook for 3–4 minutes.

3 Blend the arrowroot to a paste with 15ml/1 tbsp cold water and stir into the cherries, off the heat.

4 Return the pan to the heat and bring to the boil, stirring all the time. Cook the sauce for a minute or two, stirring until it is thick and smooth. Heat the Kirsch in a ladle over a flame, ignite and pour over the cherries. Spoon the hot sauce over scoops of ice cream and serve at once.

Apricots in Marsala

Make sure the apricots are completely covered by the syrup so that they don't discolour.

INGREDIENTS

Serves 4

12 apricots
50g/2oz/4 tbsp caster sugar
300ml/½ pint/1¼ cups Marsala
2 strips pared orange rind
1 vanilla pod, split
150ml/¼ pint/⅔ cup double or whipping cream
15ml/1 tbsp icing sugar
1.25ml/¼ tsp ground cinnamon
150ml/¼ pint/⅔ cup Greek-style yogurt

1 Halve and stone the apricots, then place in a bowl of boiling water for about 30 seconds. Drain well, then carefully slip off their skins.

2 Place the caster sugar, Marsala, orange rind, vanilla pod and 250ml/8fl oz/1 cup water in a pan. Heat gently until the sugar dissolves. Bring to the boil, without stirring, then simmer for 2–3 minutes.

3 Add the apricot halves to the pan and poach for 5–6 minutes, or until just tender. Using a slotted spoon, transfer the apricots to a serving dish.

4 Boil the syrup rapidly until reduced by half, then pour over the apricots and leave to cool. Cover and chill for several hours. Remove the orange rind and vanilla pod.

5 Whip the cream with the icing sugar and cinnamon until it forms soft peaks. Gently fold in the yogurt. Spoon into a serving bowl and chill until required. Serve with the apricots.

Plum and Port Sorbet

This is more of a sorbet for grown-ups, but you could use red grape juice in place of the port if you prefer.

INGREDIENTS 🍎

Serves 4–6

1kg/2lb ripe red plums, halved and
  stoned
75g/3oz/6 tbsp caster sugar
45ml/3 tbsp water
45ml/3 tbsp ruby port or red wine
crisp, sweet biscuits, to serve

1 Place the plums in a pan with the sugar and water. Stir over gentle heat until the sugar is melted, then cover and simmer gently for about 5 minutes, until the fruit is soft.

2 Turn into a food processor and purée until smooth, then stir in the port. Cool completely, then tip into a freezer container and freeze until firm around the edges.

3 Spoon into the food processor and process until smooth. Return to the freezer and freeze until solid.

4 Allow to soften slightly at room temperature for 15–20 minutes before serving in scoops, with crisp, sweet biscuits.

—————— COOK'S TIP ——————

You could use other fruits in place of the plums; try peaches or pears for a change.

Mango Sorbet

INGREDIENTS

Serves 6

150g/5oz caster sugar
175ml/6fl oz water
a large strip of orange rind
1 large mango, peeled, stoned, and
  cubed
60ml/4 tbsp orange juice

1 Combine the sugar, water and orange rind in a saucepan. Bring to the boil, stirring to dissolve the sugar. Leave the sugar syrup to cool.

2 Purée the mango cubes with the orange juice in a blender or food processor. There should be about 475ml/16fl oz of purée.

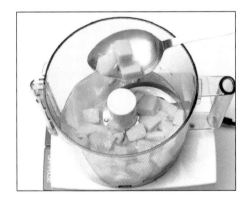

3 Add the purée to the cooled sugar syrup and mix well. Strain. Taste the mixture (it should be well flavoured). Chill.

4 When cold, tip into a freezer container and freeze until firm around the edges.

5 Spoon the semi-frozen mixture into the food processor and process until smooth. Return to the freezer and freeze until solid. Allow the sorbet to soften slightly at room temperature for 15–20 minutes before serving.

COOK'S TIP

To freeze the sorbet very quickly use a wide, shallow container and place it directly on the freezer shelf. Turn the freezer to it lowest setting about 1 hour before making the sorbet so that it has time to get really cold.

VARIATIONS

● For Banana Sorbet: peel and cube 4–5 large bananas. Purée with 30ml/2 tbsp lemon juice to make 475ml/16fl oz. If liked, replace the orange rind in the sugar syrup with 2–3 whole cloves, or omit the rind.

● For Paw Paw Sorbet: peel, seed and cube 675g/1½lb paw paw. Purée with 45ml/3 tbsp lime juice to make 475ml/16fl oz. Replace the orange rind with lime rind.

● For Passion Fruit Sorbet: halve 16 or more passion fruit and scoop out the seeds and pulp (there should be about 475ml/16fl oz). Work in a blender or food processor until the seeds are like coarse pepper. Omit the orange juice and rind. Add the passion fruit to the sugar syrup, then press through a wire sieve before freezing.

Fruit Kebabs with Mango and Yogurt Sauce

INGREDIENTS

Serves 4
½ pineapple, peeled, cored, and cubed
2 kiwi fruit, peeled and cubed
175g/6oz strawberries, hulled and cut
    in half, if large
½ mango, peeled, stoned, and cubed

For the sauce
120ml/4fl oz/½ cup fresh mango
    purée, from 1–1½ peeled and pitted
    mangoes
120ml/4fl oz/½ cup thick plain yogurt
5ml/1 tsp caster sugar
few drops vanilla essence
15ml/1 tbsp finely chopped mint
    leaves

1 To make the sauce, beat together the mango purée, yogurt, sugar and vanilla with an electric mixer.

2 Stir in the chopped mint. Cover the sauce and chill until required.

3 Thread the fruit on to twelve 15cm/6in wooden skewers, alternating the pineapple, kiwi fruit, strawberries and mango cubes.

4 Arrange the kebabs on a large serving tray with the mango and yogurt sauce in the centre.

Tropical Fruits in Cinnamon Syrup

INGREDIENTS

Serves 6
450g/1lb caster sugar
1 cinnamon stick
1 large or 2 medium paw paws, (about
    675g/1½lb), peeled, seeded and cut
    lengthways into thin pieces
1 large or 2 medium mangoes (about
    675g/1½lb), peeled, stoned, and cut
    lengthways into thin pieces
1 large or 2 small starfruit (about
    225g/8oz), thinly sliced

1 Sprinkle one-third of the sugar over the base of a large saucepan. Add the cinnamon stick and half the paw paw, mango, and starfruit pieces.

— COOK'S TIP —

Starfruit is sometimes called carambola and paw paws may also be called papayas.

2 Sprinkle half of the remaining sugar over the fruit pieces in the pan. Add the remaining fruit and sprinkle with the remaining sugar.

3 Cover the pan and cook the fruit over a medium-low heat for 35–45 minutes, until the sugar dissolves completely. Shake the pan occasionally, but do not stir or the fruit will collapse.

4 Uncover the pan and simmer until the fruit begins to appear translucent, about 10 minutes. Remove the pan from the heat and leave to cool.

5 Transfer the fruit and syrup to a bowl, cover and chill overnight.

Iced Macaroon Cream with Raspberry Sauce

Ingredients

Serves 6–8

750ml/1¼ pints double or whipping
  cream
60ml/4 tbsp brandy or orange juice
30ml/2 tbsp caster sugar
about 115g/4oz crisp almond
  macaroons, coarsely crushed
fresh raspberries, to decorate
250ml/8fl oz raspberry sauce, to serve

——————— Cook's Tip ———————

To make a quick raspberry sauce, purée about 225g/8oz fresh raspberries, then push the purée through a nylon sieve to remove the pips and sweeten to taste with icing sugar.

1 Put the cream in a large bowl, preferably chilled, and whip until it starts to thicken.

2 Add the brandy or orange juice and sugar. Continue whipping until the cream will hold stiff peaks.

3 Add the macaroons and fold evenly into the cream.

4 Spoon into six or eight ramekins, or a 1.2 litre/2 pint/5 cup smooth-sided mould. Press in evenly to be sure there are no air pockets. Smooth the surface. Cover and freeze until firm. (Do not freeze longer than 1 day.)

5 To serve, dip the moulds in hot water for 5–10 seconds, then invert on to a serving plate. Lift off the moulds. Chill the desserts for 15–20 minutes to soften slightly.

6 Decorate with raspberries and serve with the sauce.

——————— Variations ———————

You could use coarsely broken meringue nests instead of macaroons and substitute almond or Amaretto liqueur for the brandy or orange juice.

Raspberry Trifle

INGREDIENTS

Serves 6 or more

175g/6oz trifle sponges, or 2.5cm/1in
   cubes of plain Victoria sponge
   or coarsely crumbled sponge fingers.
60ml/4 tbsp medium sherry
115g/4oz raspberry jam
275g/10oz raspberries
450ml/¾ pint custard, flavoured with
   30ml/2 tbsp medium or sweet sherry
300ml/½ pint sweetened whipped
   cream
toasted flaked almonds and mint leaves,
   to decorate

1 Spread half of the sponges, cake cubes or sponge fingers over the bottom of a large serving bowl. (A glass bowl is best for presentation.)

2 Sprinkle half of the sherry over the cake to moisten it. Spoon over half of the jam, dotting it evenly over the cake cubes.

3 Reserve a few raspberries for decoration. Make a layer of half of the remaining raspberries on top.

4 Pour over half of the custard, covering the fruit and cake. Repeat the layers. Cover and chill for at least 2 hours.

VARIATION

Use other ripe summer fruit such as apricots, peaches, nectarines, and strawberries in the trifle, with jam and liqueur to suit.

5 Before serving, spoon the sweetened whipped cream evenly over the top. To decorate, sprinkle with toasted flaked almonds and arrange the reserved raspberries and the mint leaves on the top.

Fruity Ricotta Creams

Ricotta is an Italian soft cheese with a smooth texture and a mild, slightly sweet flavour. Served here with candied fruit peel and delicious chocolate – it is quite irresistible.

INGREDIENTS

Serves 4
350g/12oz/1½ cups ricotta
30–45ml/2–3 tbsp Cointreau or other orange liqueur
10ml/2 tsp grated lemon rind
30ml/2 tbsp icing sugar
150ml/¼ pint/⅔ cup double cream
150g/5oz candied peel, such as orange, lemon and citron, finely chopped
50g/2oz plain chocolate, finely chopped
chocolate curls, to decorate
amaretti biscuits, to serve (optional)

1 Using the back of a wooden spoon, push the ricotta through a fine sieve into a large bowl.

2 Add the liqueur, lemon rind and sugar to the ricotta and beat well until the mixture is light and smooth.

3 Whip the cream in a large bowl until it forms soft peaks.

4 Gently fold the cream into the ricotta mixture with the candied peel and chopped chocolate.

5 Spoon the mixture into four glass serving dishes and chill for about 1 hour. Decorate the ricotta creams with chocolate curls and serve with amaretti biscuits, if you like.

Hot Fruit with Maple Butter

INGREDIENTS

Serves 4
1 large mango
1 large paw paw
1 small pineapple
2 bananas
115g/4oz/½ cup unsalted butter
60ml/4 tbsp pure maple syrup
ground cinnamon, for sprinkling

1 Peel the mango and cut the flesh into large pieces. Halve the paw paw and scoop out the seeds. Cut into thick slices, then peel away the skin.

2 Peel and core the pineapple and slice into thin wedges. Peel the bananas then halve them lengthways.

3 Cut the butter into small dice and place in a food processor with the maple syrup, then process until the mixture is smooth and creamy.

4 Place the mango, paw paw, pineapple and banana on a grill rack and brush with the maple syrup butter.

5 Cook the fruit under a medium heat for about 10 minutes, until just tender, turning the fruit occasionally and brushing it with the butter.

6 Arrange the fruit on a warmed serving platter and dot with the remaining butter. Sprinkle over a little ground cinnamon and serve the fruit piping hot.

COOK'S TIP

Prepare the fruit just before grilling so it won't discolour. Check the label when buying maple syrup to make sure that it is 100% pure as imitations have little of the taste of the real thing.

INDEX